Sebastian Evans

The High History of the Holy Graal

Translated from the French by Sebastian Evans

.

.

.

Sebastian Evans

The High History of the Holy Graal
Translated from the French by Sebastian Evans

ISBN/EAN: 9783337285821

Printed in Europe, USA, Canada, Australia, Japan

Cover: Foto ©Lupo / pixelio.de

More available books at **www.hansebooks.com**

THE·HIGH·HISTORY
OF·THE·HOLY·GRAAL

THE HIGH
HISTORY of
THE HOLY
GRAAL

TRANSLATED
FROM THE
FRENCH BY
SEBASTIAN
EVANS
VOL. TWO

·MDCCCXCVIII·PUBLISHED·BY·J·M·DENT·
·AND·CO:·ALDINE·HOUSE·LONDON·E·C·

THE HIGH HISTORY OF
THE HOLY GRAAL

BRANCH XVI

TITLE I

THIS High History saith that Messire **Evil** Gawain and Lancelot were repaired to **tidings** the court of King Arthur from the quest they had achieved. The King made great joy thereof and the Queen. King Arthur sate one day at meat by the side of the Queen, and they had been served of the first meats. Thereupon come two knights all armed, and each bore a dead knight before him, and the knights were still armed as they had been when their bodies were alive. 'Sir,' say the knights, 'This shame and this mischief is yours. In like manner will you lose all your knights betimes and God love you not well enough to give counsel herein forthwith of His mercy.' 'Lords,' saith the King, 'How came these knights to be in so evil case?' 'Sir,' say they, 'It is of good right you ought to know. The Knight of the Fiery Dragon is entered into the head of your land, and is destroying knights and castles and whatsoever he may lay hands on, in such sort that none durst contend against him, for he is taller by a foot than any knight ever you had, and of grisly cheer, and so is his sword three times bigger than the sword of ever another knight, and his spear is well as heavy as a man may carry. Two knights might lightly cover them of his shield, and it hath on the outer side the head of a dragon that casteth forth fire and flame whensoever he will, so eager and biting that none may long endure his encounter.

II

'None other, how strong soever he be, may stand against him, and, even as you see, hath he burnt and evil-entreated all other knights that have withstood him.' 'From what land hath come such manner of man?' 'Sir,' say the knights, 'He is come from the Giant's castle, and he warreth upon you for the love of Logrin the Giant, whose head Messire Kay brought you into your court, nor never, saith he, will he have joy until such time as he shall have avenged him on your body or upon the knight that you love best.' 'Our Lord God,' saith the King, 'will defend us from so evil a man.' He is risen from the table, all scared, and maketh carry the two dead knights to be buried, and the others turn back again when they have told their message. The King calleth Messire Gawain and Lancelot and asketh them what he shall do of this knight that is entered into his land? 'By my head, I know not what to say, save you give counsel herein.' 'Sir,' saith Lancelot, 'We will go against him, so please you, I and Messire Gawain between us.' 'By my head,' saith the King, 'I would not let you go for a kingdom, for such man as is this is no knight but a devil and a fiend that hath issued from the borders of Hell. I say not but that it were great worship and prize to slay and conquer him, but he that should go against him should set his own life in right sore jeopardy and run great hazard of being in as bad plight as these two knights I have seen.' The King was in such dismay that he knew not neither what to say nor to do, and so was all the court likewise in such sort as no knight neither one nor another was minded to go to battle with him, and so remained the court in great dismay.

the Fiery Dragon

BRANCH XVII

Perceval fareth forth HERE beginneth one of the master branches of the Graal in the name of the Father, and of the Son, and of the Holy Ghost.

TITLE I

Perceval had been with his mother as long as it pleased him. He hath departed with her good will and the good will of his sister, and telleth them he will return into the land as speedily as he may. He entereth into the great Lonely Forest, and rideth so far on his journeys that he cometh one day at the right hour of noon into a passing fair launde, and seeth a forest. He looketh amidst the launde and seeth a red cross. He looketh to the head of the launde and seeth a right comely knight sitting in the shadow of the forest, and he was clad in white garments and held a vessel of gold in his hand. At the other end of the launde he seeth a damsel likewise sitting, young and gentle and of passing great beauty, and she was clad in a white samite dropped of gold. Josephus telleth us by the divine scripture that out of the forest issued a beast, white as driven snow, and it was bigger than a fox and less than a hare. The beast came into the launde all scared, for she had twelve hounds in her

8

belly, that quested within like as it were hounds **The** **Questing** **Beast**
in a wood, and she fled adown the launde for
fear of the hounds, the questing whereof she
had within her. Perceval rested on the shaft
of his spear to look at the marvel of this beast,
whereof he had right great pity, so gentle was
she of semblance, and of so passing beauty, and
by her eyes it might seem that they were two
emeralds. She runneth to the knight, all
affrighted, and when she hath been there awhile
and the hounds rend her again, she runneth to
the damsel, but neither there may she stay long
time, for the hounds that are within her cease
not of their questing, whereof is she sore adread.

II

She durst not venture herself in the forest.
She seeth Perceval and so cometh toward him
for protection. She maketh as though she
would lie down on his horse's neck, and he
holdeth forth his hands to receive her there so
as that she might not hurt herself, and evermore
the hounds quested. Howbeit the knight
crieth out to him, ' Sir Knight, let the beast go
and hold her not, for this belongeth neither to
you nor to other, but let her dree her weird.'
The beast seeth that no protection hath she.
She goeth to the cross, and forthwith might the
hounds no longer be in her, but issued forth all
as it were live hounds, but nought had they of
her gentleness nor her beauty. She humbled
herself much among them and crouched on the
ground and made semblant as though she would
have cried them mercy, and gat herself as nigh

the cross as she might. The hounds had compassed her round about and ran in upon her upon
all sides and tore her all to pieces with their
teeth, but no power had they to devour her
flesh, nor to remove it away from the cross.

III

When the hounds had all to-mangled the
beast, they fled away into the wood as had they
been raging mad. The knight and the damsel
came there where the beast lay in pieces at the
cross, and so taketh each his part and setteth
the same on their golden vessels, and took the
blood that lay upon the earth in like manner as
the flesh, and kiss the place, and adore the
cross, and then betake them into the forest.
Perceval alighteth and setteth him on his knees
before the cross and so kisseth and adoreth it,
and the place where the beast was slain, in like
manner as he had seen the knight and damsel
do; and there came to him a smell so sweet of
the cross and of the place, such as no sweetness
may be compared therewith. He looketh and
seeth coming from the forest two priests all
afoot; and the first shouteth to him: 'Sir
Knight, withdraw yourself away from the
cross, for no right have you to come nigh it':
Perceval draweth him back, and the priest
kneeleth before the cross and adoreth it and
boweth down and kisseth it more than a
score times, and manifesteth the most joy
in the world. And the other priest cometh
after, and bringeth a great rod, and setteth the

first priest aside by force, and beateth the
cross with the rod in every part, and weepeth
right passing sore.

IV

Perceval beholdeth him with right great
wonderment, and saith to him, 'Sir, herein
seem you to be no priest! wherefore do you
so great shame?' 'Sir,' saith the priest, 'It
nought concerneth you of whatsoever we may
do, nor nought shall you know thereof for us!'
Had he not been a priest, Perceval would have
been right wroth with him, but he had no will
to do him any hurt. Therewithal he departeth
and mounteth his horse and entereth the forest
again, all armed, but scarce had he ridden
away in such sort or ever he met the Knight
Coward, that cried out to him as far as he
could see him, 'Sir, for God's sake, take heed
to yourself!' 'What manner man are you?'
saith Perceval. 'Sir,' saith he, 'My name is the
Knight Coward, and I am man of the Damsel
of the Car. Wherefore I pray you for God's
sake and for your own valour that you touch
me not.' Perceval looketh on him and seeth him
tall and comely and well-shapen and adroit and
all armed upon his horse, so he saith to him,
'Sith that you are so coward, wherefore are
you armed thus?' 'Sir,' saith he, 'Against the
evil intent of any knight of whom I am adread,
for such an one might haply meet me as would
slay me forthwith.'

V

'Are you so coward as you say?' saith
Perceval. 'Yea,' saith he, 'And much more.'
'By my head,' saith he, 'I will make you
hardy. Come now along with me, for sore
pity is it that cowardice should harbour in so
comely a knight. I am fain that your name be
changed speedily, for such name beseemeth no
knight.' 'Ha, Sir, for God's sake, mercy!
Now know I well that you desire to slay me!
No will have I to change neither my courage
nor my name!' 'By my head,' saith Perceval,
'Then will you die therefor, betimes!' He
maketh him go before him, will he or nill he;
and the knight goeth accordingly with right
sore grudging. They had scarce ridden away,
when he heard in the forest off the way, two
damsels that bewailed them right sore, and
prayed our Lord God send them succour
betimes.

VI

Perceval cometh towards them, he and the
knight he driveth before him perforce, and
seeth a tall knight all armed that leadeth the
damsels all dishevelled, and smiteth them from
time to time with a great rod, so that the blood
ran down their faces. 'Ha, Sir Knight,' saith
Perceval, 'What ask you of these two damsels
that you entreat so churlishly?' 'Sir,' saith
he, 'They have disherited me of mine own hold
in this forest that Messire Gawain gave them.'
'Sir,' say they to Perceval, 'This knight is a

robber, and none other but he now wonneth in this be his
forest, for the other robber-knights were slain champion
by Messire Gawain and Lancelot and another
knight that came with them, and, for the sore
suffering and poverty that Messire Gawain and
Lancelot saw in us aforetime, and in the house
of my brother in whose castle they lay, were
they fain to give us this hold and the treasure
they conquered from the robber-knights, and
for this doth he now lead us away to slay
and destroy us, and as much would he do for
you and all other knights, so only he had the
power.' 'Sir Knight,' saith Perceval, 'Let be
these damsels, for well I know that they say
true, for that I was there when the hold was
given them.' 'Then you helped to slay my
kindred,' saith the knight, 'And therefore you
do I defy!' 'Ha,' saith the Knight Coward
to Perceval, 'Take no heed of that he saith, and
wax not wroth, but go your way!' 'Certes,'
saith Perceval, 'This will I not do: Rather
will I help to challenge the honour of the
damsels.'

VII

'Ha, Sir,' saith the Knight Coward, 'Never
shall it be challenged of me!' Perceval
draweth him back. 'Sir,' saith he, 'See here
my champion that I set in my place.' The
robber-knight moveth toward him, and smiteth
him so sore on the shield that he breaketh his
spear, but he might not unseat the Coward
Knight, that sate still upright as aforehand in
the saddle-bows. He looketh at the other

knight that hath drawn his sword. The Knight Coward looketh on the one side and the other, and would fain have fled and he durst. But Perceval crieth to him: 'Knight, do your endeavour to save my honour and your own life and the honour of these two damsels!' And the robber-knight dealeth him a great buffet of his sword so as that it went nigh to stun him altogether. Howbeit the Coward Knight moveth not. Perceval looketh at him in wonderment and thinketh him that he hath set too craven a knight in his place, and now at last knoweth well that he spake truth. The robber-knight smiteth him all over his body and giveth him so many buffets that the knight seeth his own blood. 'By my head,' saith he, 'You have wounded me, but you shall pay there-for, for I supposed not that you were minded to slay me!' He draweth his sword, that was sharp and strong, and smiteth his horse right sore hard of his spurs, and catcheth the knight with his sword right in the midst of his breast with a sweep so strong that he beareth him to the ground beside his horse. He alighteth over him, unlaceth his ventail and smiteth down his coif, then striketh off his head and presenteth it to Perceval. 'Sir,' saith he, 'Here give I you of my first joust.' 'By my head,' said Perceval, 'Right dearly love I this present! Now take heed that you never again fall back into the cowardice wherein you have been. For it is too sore shame to a knight!' 'Sir,' saith he, 'I will not, but never should I have believed that one could become hardy so speedily, or

otherwise long ago would I have become so, **becometh**
and so should I have had worship and honour **the**
thereof, for many a knight hath held me in **Knight**
contempt herein, that elsewise would · have **Hardy**
honoured me.' Perceval answereth that right
and reason it is that worshipful men should be
more honoured than the other. 'I commend
these two damsels to your protection, and lead
them to their hold in safety, and be at their
pleasure and their will, and so say everywhere
that you have for name the Knight Hardy, for
more of courtesy hath this name than the other.'
'Sir,' saith he, 'You say true, and you have I
to thank for the name.' The damsels give
great thanks to Perceval, and take leave of
him, and so go their way with right good will
toward the knight that goeth with them on
account of the knight he had slain, so that
thereof called they him the Knight Hardy.

VIII

Perceval departeth from the place where
the knight lieth dead, and rideth until that he
draweth nigh to Cardoil where King Arthur
was, and findeth the country round in sore
terror and dismay. Much he marvelleth
wherefor it may be, and demandeth of some
of the meaner sort wherefore they are in so
sore affright. 'Doth the King, then, live no
longer?' 'Sir,' say the most part, 'Yea, he
is there within in this castle, but never was he
so destroyed nor so scared as he is at this
present. For a knight warreth upon him

against whom no knight in the world may endure.' Perceval rideth on until he cometh before the master hall, and is alighted on the mounting-stage. Lancelot and Messire Gawain come to meet him and make much joy of him, as do the King and Queen and all they of the court; and they made disarm him and do upon him a right rich robe. They that had never seen him before looked upon him right fainly for the worship and valour of his knighthood. The court also was rejoiced because of him, for sore troubled had it been. So as the King sate one day at meat, there came four knights into the hall, and each one of them bore before him a dead knight. And their feet and arms had been stricken off, but their bodies were still all armed, and the habergeons thereon were all black as though they had been blasted of lightning. They laid the knights in the midst of the hall. 'Sir,' say they to the King, 'Once more is made manifest this shame that is done you that is not yet amended. The Knight of the Dragon destroyeth you your land and slayeth your men and cometh as nigh us as he may, and saith that in your court shall never be found knight so hardy as that he durst abide him or assault him.' Right sore shame hath the King of these tidings, and Messire Gawain and Lancelot likewise. Right sorrowful are they of heart for that the King would not allow them to go thither. The four knights turn back again and leave the dead knights in the hall, but the King maketh them be buried with the others.

IX

A great murmuring ariseth amongst the
knights in the hall, and the most part say
plainly that they never heard tell of none that
slew knights in such cruel sort, nor so many as
did he; and that neither Messire Gawain nor
Lancelot ought to be blamed for that they went
not thither, for no knight in the world might
conquer such a man and our Lord God did not,
for he casteth forth fire and flame from his
shield whensoever him listeth. And while this
murmur was going on between the knights all
round about the hall, behold you therewithal
the Damsel that made bear the knight in the
horse-bier and cometh before the King. 'Sir,'
saith she, 'I pray and beseech you that you
do me right in your court. See, here is Messire
Gawain that was at the assembly in the Red
Launde where were many knights, and among
them was the son of the Widow Lady, that I
see sitting beside you. He and Messire Gawain
were they that won the most prize of the
assembly. This knight had white arms, and
they of the assembly said that he had better
done than Messire Gawain, for that he had been
first in the assembly. It had been granted me,
before the assembly began, that he that should
do best thereat, should avenge the knight. Sir,
I have sought for him until I have now found
him at your court. Wherefore I pray and
beseech you that you bid him do so much
herein as that he be not blamed, for Messire
Gawain well knoweth that I have spoken true.

But the knight departed so soon from the
assembly, that I knew not what had become of
him, and Messire Gawain was right heavy for
that he had departed, for he was in quest of
him, but knew him not.'

X

'Damsel,' saith Messire Gawain, 'Truth it
is that he it was that did best at the assembly in
the Red Launde, and moreover, please God,
well will he fulfil his covenant towards you.'
'Messire Gawain,' saith Perceval, 'Meseemeth
you did best above all other.' 'By my faith,'
saith Messire Gawain, 'You speak of your
courtesy, but howsoever I or other may have
done, you had the prize therein by the judgment of the knights. Of so much may I well
call upon the damsel to bear witness.' 'Sir,'
saith she, 'Gramercy! He ought not to deny
me that I require of him. For the knight that
I have so long followed about and borne on a
bier was son of his uncle Elinant of Escavalon.'

XI

'Damsel,' saith Perceval, 'Take heed that
you speak truth. I know well that Elinant of
Escavalon was my uncle on my father's side,
but of his son know I nought.' 'Sir,' saith
she, 'Of his deeds well deserved he to be
known, for by his great valour and hardiment
came he by his death, and he had to name
Alein of Escavalon. The Damsel of the
Circlet of Gold loved him of passing great love
with all her might. The comeliest knight that

was ever seen of his age was he, and had he lived longer would have been one of the best knights known, and of the great love she had in him made she his body be embalmed when the Knight of the Dragon had slain him, he that is so cruel and maketh desolate all the lands and all the islands. The Damsel of the Circlet of Gold hath he defied in such sort that already hath he slain great part of her knights, and she is held fast in her castle, so that she durst not issue forth, insomuch that all the knights that are there say, and the Lady of the castle also, that he that shall avenge this knight shall have the Circlet of Gold, that never before was she willing to part withal, and the fairest guerdon will that be that any knight may have.

XII

'Sir,' saith she, 'Well behoveth you, therefore, to do your best endeavour to avenge your uncle's son, and to win the Circlet of Gold, for, and you slay the knight, you will have saved the land of King Arthur that he threateneth to make desolate, and all the lands that march with his own, for no King hateth he so much as King Arthur on account of the head of the Giant whereof he made such joy at his court.' 'Damsel,' saith Perceval, 'Where is the Knight of the Dragon?' 'Sir,' saith she, 'He is in the isles of the Elephants that wont to be the fairest land and the richest in the world. Now hath he made it all desolate, they say, in such sort that none durst inhabit there, and the

The island wherein he abideth is over against the three castle of the Damsel of the Golden Circlet, so best that every day she seeth him carry knights off knights bodily from the forest that he slayeth and smiteth limb from limb, whereof hath she right sore grief at heart.'

XIII

Perceval heareth this that the damsel telleth him, and marvelleth much thereat, and taketh thought within himself, sith that the adventure is thus thrown upon him, that great blame will he have thereof and he achieve it not. He taketh leave of the King and Queen, and so goeth his way and departeth from the Court. Messire Gawain departeth and Lancelot with him, and say they will bear him company to the piece of ground, and they may go thither. Perceval holdeth their fellowship right dear. The King and Queen have great pity of Perceval, and say all that never until now no knight went into jeopardy so sore, and that sore loss to the world will it be if there he should die. They send to all the hermits and worshipful men in the forest of Cardoil and bid them pray for Perceval that God defend him from this enemy with whom he goeth forth to do battle. Lancelot and Messire Gawain go with him by the strange forests and by the islands, and found the forests all void and desolate and wasted in place after place. The Damsel followeth them together with the dead knight. And so far have they wandered that they come into the plain country before the forest. So they looked before them and saw a castle that **The** was seated in the plain without the forest, and **Castle** they saw that it was set in a right fair meadow- **of En-** land and was surrounded of great running waters **deavour** and girdled of high walls, and had within great halls with windows. They draw nigh the castle and see that it turneth all about faster than the wind may run, and it had at the top the archers of crossbows of copper that draw their shafts so strong that no armour in the world might avail against the stroke thereof. Together with them were men of copper that turned and sounded their horns so passing loud that the ground all seemed to quake. And under the gateway were lions and bears chained, that roared with so passing great might and fury that all the ground and the valley resounded thereof. The knights draw rein and look at this marvel. 'Lords,' saith the damsel, 'Now may you see the Castle of Great Endeavour. Messire Gawain and Lancelot, draw you back, and come not nigher the archers, for otherwise ye be but dead men. And you, Sir,' saith she to Perceval, 'And you would enter into this castle, lend me your spear and shield, and so will I bear them before for warranty, and you come after me and make such countenance as good knight should, and so shall you pass through into the castle. But your fellows may well draw back, for now is not the hour for them to pass. None may pass thither save only he that goeth to vanquish the knight and win the Golden Circlet and the Graal, and do away the false law with its horns of copper.'

XIV

Perceval is right sorrowful when he heareth the damsel say that Messire Gawain and Lancelot may not pass in thither with him albeit they are the best knights in the world. He taketh leave of them full sorrowfully, and they also depart sore grudgingly; but they pray him right sweetly, so Lord God allow him escape alive from the place whither he goeth, that he will meet them again at some time and place, and at ease, in such sort as that they may see him without discognisance. They wait awhile to watch the Good Knight, that hath yielded his shield and spear to the damsel. She hath set his shield on the bier in front, then pointeth out to them of the castle all openly the shield that belonged to the Good Soldier; after that, she maketh sign that it belongeth to the knight that is there waiting behind her. Perceval was without shield in the saddle-bows, and holdeth his sword drawn and planteth him stiffly in the stirrups after such sort as maketh them creak again and his horse's chine swerve awry. After that, he looketh at Lancelot and Messire Gawain. 'Lords,' saith he, 'To the Saviour of the World commend I you.' And they answer, 'May He that endured pain of His body on the Holy True Cross protect him in his body and his soul and his life.' With that he smiteth with his spurs and goeth his way to the castle as fast as his horse may carry him,—toward the Turning Castle. He smiteth with his sword at the gate so

passing strongly that he cut a good three fingers Perceval
into a shaft of marble. The lions and the entereth
beast that were chained to guard the gate slink there-
away into their dens and the castle stoppeth at into
once. The archers cease to shoot. There
were three bridges before the castle that up-
lifted themselves so soon as he was beyond.

XV

Lancelot and Messire Gawain departed
thence when they had beholden the marvel,
but they were fain to go toward the castle when
they saw it stop turning. But a knight cried
out to them from the battlements, 'Lords, and
you come forward, the archers will shoot and
the castle will turn, and the bridges be lowered
again, wherefore you would be deceived herein.'
They draw back, and hear made within the
greatest joy that ever was heard, and they hear
how the most part therewithin say that now is
he come of whom they shall be saved in twofold
wise,—saved as of life, and saved as of soul, so
God grant him to vanquish the knight that
beareth the spirit of the devil. Lancelot and
Messire Gawain turn them back thoughtful
and all heavy for that they may not pass into
the castle, for none other passage might they
see than this. So they ride on, until that they
draw nigh the Waste City where Lancelot slew
the knight. 'Ha,' saith he to Messire Gawain,
'Now is the time at hand that behoveth me to
die in this Waste City, and God grant not
counsel herein.' He told Messire Gawain all
the truth of that which had befallen him therein.

Lancelot is re-spited So, even as he would have taken leave of him, behold you, the Poor Knight of the Waste Castle!

XVI

'Sir,' saith he to Lancelot, 'I have taken respite of you in the city within there, of the knight that you slew, until forty days after that the Graal shall be achieved, nor have I issued forth of the castle wherein you harboured you until now, nor should I now have come forth had I not seen you come for fulfilling of your pledge, nor never shall I come forth again until such time as you shall return hither on the day I have named to you. And so, gramercy to you and Messire Gawain for the horses you sent me, that were a right great help to us, and for the treasure and the hold you have given to my sisters that were sore poverty-stricken. But I may not do otherwise than abide in my present poverty until such time as you shall be returned, on the day whereunto I have taken respite for you, sore against the will of your enemies, for the benefits you have done me. Wherefore I pray you forget me not, for the saving of your loyalty.' 'By my head,' saith Lancelot, 'That will I not, and gramercy for having put off the day for love of me.' They depart from the knight and come back again toward Cardoil where King Arthur was.

HERE the story is silent of Lancelot and Messire Gawain, and saith that Perceval is in the Turning Castle, whereof Joseus recounteth the truth, to wit, that Virgil founded it in the air by his wisdom in such fashion, when the philosophers went on the Quest of the Earthly Paradise, and it was prophesied that the castle should not cease turning until such time as the Knight should come thither that should have a head of gold, the look of a lion, a heart of steel, the navel of a virgin maiden, conditions without wickedness, the valour of a man and faith and belief of God; and that this knight should bear the shield of the Good Soldier that took down the Saviour of the World from hanging on the rood. It was prophesied, moreover, that all they of the castle and all other castles whereof this one was the guardian should hold the old law until such time as the Good Knight should come, by whom their souls should be saved and their death respited. For, so soon as he should be come, they should run to be baptized and should firmly believe the new law. Wherefore was the joy great in the castle for that their death should now be respited, and that they

Virgil his craft

should be released of all terror of the knight that was their foe, whom they dreaded even to the death, and of the sin of the false law whereof they had heretofore been attaint.

II

Right glad is Perceval when he seeth the people of the castle turn them to the holy faith of the Saviour, and the damsel saith to him, 'Sir, right well have you speeded thus far on your way; nought is there now to be done save to finish that which remaineth. For never may they that are within issue forth so long as the Knight of the Dragon is on live. Here may you not tarry, for the longer you tarry, the more lands will be desolate and the more folk will he slay.' Perceval taketh leave of them of the castle, that make much joy of him, but sore misgiving have they of him on account of the knight with whom he goeth to do battle, and they say that if he shall conquer him, never yet befell knight so fair adventure. They have heard mass before that he departeth, and made rich offerings for him in honour of the Saviour and His sweet Mother. The damsel goeth before, for that she knew the place where the evil knight had his repair. They ride until they come into the Island of Elephants. The Knight was alighted under an olive tree, and had but now since slain four knights that were of the castle of the Queen of the Golden Circlet. She was at the windows of her castle and saw her knights dead, whereof made she great dole. 'Ha, God,' saith she, 'Shall I never see none

that may avenge me of this evil-doer that slayeth **The**
my men and destroyeth my land on this wise?' **Queen**
She looketh up and seeth Perceval come and **of the**
the damsel. 'Sir Knight, and you have not **Circlet**
force and help and valour in you more than is
in four knights, come not nigh this devil!
Howbeit, and you feel that you may so do
battle as to overcome and vanquish him, I will
give you the Golden Circlet that is within, and
will hold with the New Law that hath been
of late established. For I see well by your
shield that you are a Christian, and, so you may
conquer him, then ought I at last to be assured
that your law availeth more than doth ours,
and that God was born of the Virgin.'

III

Right joyous is Perceval of this that he
heareth her say. He crosseth and blesseth
him, and commendeth him to God and His
sweet Mother, and is pricked of wrath and
hardiment like a lion. He seeth the Knight of
the Dragon mounted, and looketh at him in
wonderment, for that he was so big that never
had he seen any man so big of his body. He
seeth the shield at his neck, that was right
black and huge and hideous. He seeth the
Dragon's head in the midst thereof, that casteth
out fire and flame in great plenty, so foul and
hideous and horrible that all the field stank
thereof. The damsel draweth her toward the
castle and leaveth the knight on the horse-bier
nigh the plain.

IV

'Sir,' saith she to Perceval, 'On this level
plot was slain your uncle's son whom here I
leave, for I have brought him far enough.
Now avenge him as best you may, I render and
give him over to you, for so much have I done
herein as that none hath right to blame me.'
With that she departeth. The Knight of the
Dragon removeth and seeth Perceval coming
all alone, wherefore hath he great scorn of him
and deigneth not to take his spear, but rather
cometh at him with his drawn sword, that was
right long and red as a burning brand. Perceval
seeth him coming and goeth against him, spear
in rest, as hard as his horse may carry him,
thinking to smite him through the breast. But
the Knight setteth his shield between, and the
flame that issued from the Dragon burnt the shaft
thereof even to his hand. And the Knight
smiteth him on the top of his helmet, but
Perceval covereth him of his shield, whereof
had he great affiance that the sword of the
foeman knight might not harm it. Josephus
witnesseth us that Joseph of Abarimacie had
made be sealed in the boss of the shield some
of the blood of Our Lord and a piece of His
garment.

V

When the Knight seeth that he hath not
hurt Perceval's shield, great marvel hath he
thereof, for never aforetime had he smitten
knight but he had dealt him his death-blow.

He turneth the head of the Dragon toward **Burning** Perceval's shield, but the flame that issued from **Dragon** the Dragon's head turned back again as had it been blown of the wind, so that it might not come nigh him. The Knight is right wroth thereof, and passeth beyond and cometh to the bier of the dead knight and turneth his shield with the dragon's head against him. He scorcheth and burneth all to ashes the bodies of the knight and the horses. Saith he to Perceval, 'Are you quit as for this knight's burial?' 'Certes,' saith Perceval, 'You say true, and much misliketh me thereof, but please God, I shall amend it.'

VI

The damsel that had brought the knight was at the windows of the palace beside the Queen. She crieth out. 'Perceval, fair sir,' saith the damsel, 'Now is the shame the greater and the harm the greater, and you amend them not.' Right sorrowful is Perceval of his cousin that is all burnt to a cinder, and he seeth the Knight that beareth the devil with him, but knoweth not how he may do vengeance upon him. He cometh to him sword drawn, and dealeth him a great blow on the shield in such sort that he cleaveth it right to the midst thereof where the dragon's head was, and the flame leapeth forth so burning hot on his sword that it waxed red-hot like as was the Knight's sword. And the damsel crieth to him : 'Now is your sword of the like power as his ; now shall it be seen what you will do! I have been

told of a truth that the Knight may not be
vanquished save by one only and at one blow,
but how this is I may not tell, whereof irketh
me.' Perceval looketh and seeth that his
sword is all in a flame of fire, whereof much
he marvelleth. He smiteth the Knight so
passing sore that he maketh his head stoop
down over the fore saddle-bow. The Knight
righteth him again, sore wrath that he may not
put him to the worse. He smiteth him with
his sword a blow so heavy that he cleaveth the
habergeon and his right shoulder so as that he
cutteth and burneth the flesh to the bone. As
he draweth back his blow, Perceval catcheth
him and striketh with such passing strength
that he smiteth off his hand, sword and all.
The Knight gave a great roar, and the Queen
was right joyous thereof. The Knight natheless
made no semblant that he was yet conquered,
but turneth back toward Perceval at a right
great gallop and launcheth his flame against his
shield, but it availeth him nought, for he might
not harm it. Perceval seeth the dragon's head,
that was broad and long and horrible, and
aimeth with his sword and thrusteth it up to the
hilt into his gullet as straight as ever he may,
and the head of the dragon hurleth forth a cry so
huge that forest and fell resound thereof as far
as two leagues Welsh.

VII

The dragon's head turneth it toward his
lord in great wrath, and scorcheth him and
burneth him to dust, and thereafter departeth

up into the sky like lightning. The Queen
cometh to Perceval, and all the knights, and
see that he is sore hurt in his right shoulder.
And the damsel telleth him that never will he
he healed thereof save he setteth thereon of the
dust of the knight that is dead. And they lead
him up to the castle with right great joy.
Then they make him be disarmed, and have his
wound washed and tended and some of the
knight's dust that was dead set thereon that it
might have healing. She maketh send to all
the knights of her land : 'Lords,' saith she,
' See here the knight that hath saved my land
for me and protected your lives. You know
well how it hath been prophesied that the knight
with head of gold should come, and that through
him should you be saved. And now, behold,
hath he come hither. The prophecy may not
be belied. I will that you do his commandment.' And they said that so would they do
right willingly. She bringeth him there where
the Circlet of Gold is, and she herself setteth
it on his head. After that, she bringeth his
sword and delivereth it unto him, wherewith he
had slain the giant devil, both the knight that
bare the devil and the devil that the knight
bare in his shield.

VIII

' Sir,' saith she, ' May all they that will not
go to be baptized, nor accept your New Law,
be slain of this your sword, and hereof I make
you the gift.' She herself made her be held
up and baptized first, and all the other after.

Josephus maketh record that in right baptism
she had for name Elysa, and a good life she
led and right holy, and she died a virgin. Her
body still lieth in the kingdom of Ireland, where
she is highly honoured. Perceval was within
the castle until that he was heal. The tidings
spread throughout the lands that the Knight of
the Golden Circlet had slain the Knight of the
Dragon, and great everywhere was the joy
thereof. It was known at the court of King
Arthur, but much marvelled they that it was
said the Knight of the Golden Circlet had slain
him, for they knew not who was the Knight of
the Golden Circlet.

IX

When Perceval was whole, he departed from
the castle of the Queen of the Golden Circlet,
all of whose land was at his commandment.
The Queen told him that she would keep the
Golden Circlet until he should will otherwise,
and in such sort he left it there, for he would
not carry it with him, sith that he knew not
whitherward he might turn. The history
telleth us that he rode on until one day he
came to the Castle of Copper. Within the
castle were a number of folk that worshipped
the bull of copper and believed not in any other
God. The bull of copper was in the midst of
the castle upon four columns of copper, and
bellowed so loud at all hours of the day that it
was heard for a league all round about, and
there was an evil spirit within that gave answers
concerning whatsoever any should ask of it.

X

At the entrance to the gateway of the castle
were two men made of copper by the art of
nigromancy, and they held two great mallets of
iron, and they busied themselves striking the
one after the other, and so strongly they struck
that nought mortal is there in the world that
might pass through amongst their blows but
should be all to-crushed thereby. And on the
other side was the castle so fast enclosed about
that nought might enter thereinto.

XI

Perceval beholdeth the fortress of the castle,
and the entrance that was so perilous, whereof
he marvelleth much. He passeth a bridge that
was within the entry, and cometh nigh them
that guard the gate. A Voice began to cry
aloud above the gate that he might go forward
safely, and that he need have no care for the
men of copper that guarded the gate nor be
affrighted of their blows, for no power had
they to harm such a knight as was he He
comforteth himself much of that the Voice
saith to him. He cometh anigh the serjeants
of copper, and they cease to strike at once, and
hold their iron mallets quite still. And he
entereth into the castle, where he findeth within
great plenty of folk that all were misbelievers
and of feeble belief. He seeth the bull of
copper in the midst of the castle right big and
horrible, that was surrounded on all sides by
folk that all did worship thereunto together
round about.

XII

The bull bellowed so passing loud that right uneath was it to hear aught else within the castle besides. Perceval was therewithin, but none was there that spake unto him, for so intent were they upon adoring the bull that, and any had been minded to slay them what time they were yet worshipping the same, they would have allowed him so to do and would have thought that they were saved thereby; and save this had they none other believe in the world. It was not of custom within there to be armed, for the entrance of the fortress was so strong that none might enter but by their will and commandment, save it were the pleasure of our Lord God. And the devil that had deceived them, and in whom they believed, gave them such great abundance therewithin of everything they could desire, that nought in the world was there whereof they lacked. When he perceived that they held no discourse with him, he draweth himself on one side by a great hall, and so called them around him. The more part came thither, but some of them came not. The Voice warneth him that he make them all pass through the entrance of the gateway there where the men with the iron mallets are, for there may he well prove which of them are willing to believe in God and which not. The Good Knight draweth his sword and surroundeth them all and maketh them all go in common before him, would they or nould they. And they that would not go willingly and kindly might be sure that they should receive their death. He made them pass through the entrance there where the serjeants of copper were striking great blows with their iron mallets. Of one thousand five hundred that there were, scarce but thirteen were not all slain and brained of the iron mallets. But the thirteen had firmly bound their belief in Our Lord, wherefore the serjeants took no heed of them.

XIII

The evil spirit that was in the bull of copper issued forth thereof as it had been lightning from heaven, and the bull of copper melted all in a heap so as that nought remained in that place thereof. Then the thirteen that remained sent for a hermit of the forest and so made themselves be held up and baptized   After that, they took the bodies of the misbelievers and made cast them into a water that is called the River of Hell. This water runneth into the sea, so say many that have seen it, and there where it spendeth itself in the sea is it most foul and most horrible, so that scarce may ship pass that is not wrecked.

XIV

Josephus maketh record that the hermit that baptized the thirteen had the name of Denis, and that the castle was named the Castle of the Trial. They lived within there until the New Law was assured and believed in throughout all the kingdoms, and a right good life led they and

King a holy.   Nor never might none enter with them
Hermit thereinto but was slain and crushed save he
firmly believed in God.   When the thirteen
that were baptized in the castle issued forth
thereof they scattered themselves on every side
among strange forests, and made hermitages and
buildings, and put their bodies to penance for the
false law they had maintained and to win the
love of the Saviour of the World.

XV

Perceval, as you may hear, was soldier of
Our Lord, and well did God show him how He
loved his knighthood, for the Good Knight had
much pain and sore travail and pleased Him
greatly.   He was come one day to the house
of King Hermit that much desired to see him,
and made much joy of him when he saw him,
and rejoiced greatly of his courage.   Perceval
relateth to him all the greater adventures that
have befallen him at many times and in many
places sithence that he departed from him, and
King Hermit much marvelleth him of many.
'Uncle,' saith Perceval, 'I marvel me much of
an adventure that befell me at the outlet of a
forest; for I saw a little white beast that I
found in the launde of the forest, and twelve
hounds had she in her belly, that bayed aloud
and quested within her.   At last they issued
forth of her and slew her beside the cross that
was at the outlet of the forest, but they might
not eat of her flesh.   A knight and a damsel,
whereof one was at one end of the launde and

the other at the other, came thither and took the **King** flesh and the blood, and set them in two vessels **Hermit** of gold. And the hounds that were born of **preacheth** her fled away into the forest.' 'Fair nephew,' saith the Hermit, 'I know well that God loveth you sith that such things appear to you, for His valour and yours and for the chastity that is in your body. The beast, that was kindly and gentle and sweet, signifieth Our Lord Jesus Christ, and the twelve dogs that yelped within her signify the people of the Old Law that God created and made in His own likeness, and after that He had made and created them He desired to prove how much they loved Him. He sent them forty years into the wilderness, where their garments never wasted, and sent them manna from heaven that served them whatsoever they would to eat and to drink, and they were without evil and without trouble and without sickness, and such joy and pleasance had they as they would. And they held one day their council, and the master of them said that and God should wax wroth with them and withhold this manna, they would have nought to eat, and that it might not last always albeit that God sent it in so passing great plenty. Wherefore they purposed to set aside great part thereof in store, so that if the Lord God should wax wroth they might take of that which was stored and so save themselves for a long space. They agreed among themselves and did thereafter as they had purposed and determined amongst them.

XVI

'God, that seeth and knoweth all things, knew well their thought. He withdrew from them the manna from heaven that had come to them in such abundance, and which they had bestowed in caverns underground, thinking to find there the manna they had set aside, but it was changed by the will of God into efts and adders and worms and vermin, and when they saw that they had done evil, they scattered themselves over strange lands. Fair, sweet nephew,' saith the Hermit, 'These twelve hounds that bayed in the beast are the Jews that God had fed, and that were born in the Law that He established, nor never would they believe on Him, nor love Him, but rather crucified Him and tore His Body after the shamefullest sort they might, but in no wise might they destroy His flesh. The knight and damsel that set the pieces of flesh in vessels of gold signify the divinity of the Father, which would not that His flesh should be minished. The hounds fled to the forest and became savage what time they had torn the beast to pieces, so in like manner are the Jews that were and ever shall be savage, subject to them of the New Law henceforth for ever.'

XVII

'Fair uncle,' saith Perceval, 'Good right and reason is it that they should have shame and tribulation and evil reward sith that they slew and crucified Him that had created and made them and deigned to be born as a man in their Law. But two priests came after, whereof the one kissed the cross and worshipped it right **Of the** heartily and made great joy thereof, and the **two** other did violence thereunto and beat it with a **priests** great rod, and wept right sore and made the greatest dole in the world.   With this last was I right sore wrath, and willingly would I have run upon him had he not been a priest.'   'Fair nephew,' saith the Hermit, 'He that beat it believed in God equally as well as he that adored, for that the holy flesh of the Saviour of the World was set thereon, that abhorred not the pains of death.   One smiled and made great joy for that He redeemed His souls from the pains of hell that would otherwise have been therein for evermore ; and for this made he yet greater joy, that he knew He was God and Man everlastingly in His nature, for he that hath not this in remembrance shall never believe aright. Fair nephew, the other priest beat the cross and wept for the passing great anguish and torment and dolour that our Lord God suffered thereon, for so sore was the anguish as might have melted the rock, nor no tongue of man may tell the sorrow He felt upon the cross.   And therefore did he beat it and revile it for that He was crucified thereon, even as I might hate a spear or sword wherewith you had been slain.   For nought else did he thus, and ever, so often as he remembereth the pain that God suffered thereon, cometh he to the cross in such manner as you saw.   Both twain are hermits and dwell in the forest, and he is named Jonas that kissed and adored the cross, and he that beat and reviled it is named Alexis.'

XVIII

Willingly heareth Perceval this that his uncle telleth and recordeth him. He relateth how he did battle with the devil-knight that bare in his shield the head of a dragon that cast forth fire and flame, and how the dragon burnt up his lord at the last. 'Fair nephew,' saith the Hermit, 'Right glad am I of these tidings that you tell me, for I have been borne on hand that the Knight of the Golden Circlet had slain him.' 'Sir,' saith Perceval, 'It may well be, but never at any time saw I knight so big and horrible.' 'Fair nephew,' saith the Hermit, 'None might overcome him save the Good Knight only, for all true worshipful men behoveth do battle with the Devil, nor never may he be worshipful man that fighteth not against him. And even as the devil withal that was figured on his shield slew and burnt up his master, even so doth one devil torment and molest other in the world to come; and greater evil might not the Knight of the Devil do you than burn the body of your uncle's son that he had killed, as I have heard tell. Power had he over his body, but, please God, not over his soul to burn it.' 'Fair uncle,' saith Perceval, 'I went thither by a Turning Castle, where were archers of copper that shot bolts, and bears and lions chained at the entrance of the gateway. So soon as I drew nigh and smote thereon with my sword the castle stopped still.' 'Fair nephew,' saith King Hermit, 'Nought had the Devil outwardly besides this castle. It was the entrance to his fortress, nor would they within ever have been converted save you had been there.' 'Sir,' saith he, 'Right sorrowful am I of Messire Gawain and Lancelot, for well I loved their fellowship, and great aid would they have been in my need.' 'Fair nephew, had they been chaste as are you, well might they have entered on account of their good knighthood. For were they not wanton, the two best knights in the world are they.

XIX

'Fair nephew, in the time of your knighthood have you much advanced the Law of the Saviour, for you have destroyed the falsest believe in the world, and this was of them that believed on the bull of copper and the devil that was therein. If this folk had remained, and had failed of you, never would it have been destroyed until the end of the world. Wherefore marvel not that you have travail in serving God, but endure it willingly, for never had worshipful man honour without pains. But now behoveth you achieve another matter. All they of the land of King Fisherman your uncle have abandoned the New Law, and returned to that which God hath forbidden. But the most part do so rather perforce and for fear of the King that hath seized the land, who is my brother and your uncle, than on account of aught else. Wherefore behoveth you set counsel therein, for this thing may not be achieved by any earthly man save by you

The only. For the castle and land should be yours
Castle of right, and sore mischief is it when one that
of the cometh of lineage so high and so holy is traitor
Graal to God, and disloyal to the world.

XX

'Fair nephew,' saith the good man, 'The
castle hath been much strengthened, for there
are now nine bridges newly made, and at each
bridge are there three knights tall and strong
and hardy, whereof hath he much defence, and
your uncle is there within that keepeth the
castle. But never sithence, none of the knights
of King Fisherman nor of his priests have there
appeared, nor knoweth any what hath befallen
them. The chapel where the most Holy Graal
appeared is all emptied of its sacred hallows;
the hermits that are by the forest are fain of
your coming, for never see they there a knight
pass by that believeth in God. And, so you
shall have achieved this enterprise, it is a thing
whereof shall God be well pleased.'

XXI

'Fair uncle,' saith Perceval, 'Thither will I
go, sith that you commend it to me, for no
reason is it that he should have the castle that
hath entered thereinto. Of better right ought
my mother to have it, that was the next-born
to King Fisherman, of whose death am I right
sorrowful.' 'Fair nephew, you are right! for
on your account fell he into languishment, and,
had you then gone again, so say many, then
would he have been whole, but how this might

have been I know not of a certainty. But methinketh our Lord God willed his languishment
and death, for had it been His will, you would
have made the demand, but He willed otherwise, wherefore ought we to give thanks and
praise Him whatsoever He doth, for He hath
foreseen of every man that which shall come to
him. I have within here a white mule that is
very old. Fair nephew, you will take her with
you. She will follow you right willingly, and
a banner shall you bear, for the power of God
and His virtue shall avail more than your own.
Seven-and-twenty knights guard the nine bridges,
all chosen and of approved great valour, and
none ought now to believe that a single knight
may vanquish so many, save the miracle of Our
Lord and His virtue shall open a way for him.
So I pray and beseech you that you have God
always in remembrance and His sweet Mother,
and, so at any time you be put to the worse of
your knighthood, mount upon the mule and
take the banner, and your enemies shall forthwith lose their force, for nought confoundeth
any enemy so swiftly as doth the virtue and
puissance of God. It is a thing well known
that you are the Best Knight of the World, but
set not affiance in your strength nor in your
knighthood as against so many knights, for
against them may you not endure.'

King Hermit's discourse

XXII

Perceval hearkeneth to his uncle's discourse
and his chastening, and layeth fast hold on all
that he saith, wherewith is he pleased full well,

for great affiance hath he in his words.   'Fair
nephew,' saith the Hermit, 'Two lions are
there at the entry of the gateway, whereof the
one is red and the other white.   Put your trust
in the white, for he is on God's side, and look
at him whensoever your force shall fail you,
and he will look at you likewise in such sort as
that straightway you shall know his intent, by
the will and pleasure of Our Saviour.   Wherefore do according as you shall see that he
would, for no intent will he have save good
only, and to help you; nor may you not
otherwise succeed in winning past the nine
bridges that are warded of the twenty-seven
knights.   And God grant you may win past in
such wise that you may save your body and set
forward withal the Law of Our Lord that your
uncle hath hindered all that he might.'

XXIII

Perceval departeth from the hermitage, and
carrieth away the banner, according to his
uncle's counsel, and the white mule followeth
after.   He goeth his way toward the land that
was the land of King Fisherman, and findeth a
hermit that was issued forth of his hermitage
and was going at a great pace through the
forest.   He abideth so soon as he beholdeth
the cross on Perceval's shield.   'Sir,' saith
he, 'I well perceive that you are a Christian,
of whom not a single one have I seen this long
time past.   For the King of Castle Mortal is
driving us forth of this forest, for he hath

renounced God and His sweet Mother, so that **Hermits**
we durst not remain in His defence.'   'By my **in exile**
faith,' saith Perceval, 'But you shall! for God
shall lead you forward, and I after.   Are there
more hermits in this forest?' saith Perceval.
'Yea, Sir, there be twelve here that are waiting
for me at a cross yonder before us, and we are
minded to go to the kingdom of Logres and put
our bodies to penance for God's sake, and to
abandon our cells and chapels in this forest for
dread of this felon King that hath seized the
land, for he willeth that none who believeth in
God should here abide.'

XXIV

Perceval is come with the hermit to the cross
where the good men had assembled them together, and findeth Joseus, the young man that
was King Pelles' son, of whom he maketh
right great joy, and he maketh the hermits turn
back again with him, saying that he will defend
them and make them safe, by God's help, in the
kingdom, and prayeth them right sweetly that
they make prayer for him to our Lord that He
grant him to win back that which of right is
his own.   He is come forth of the forest and
the hermits with him.   He draweth nigh to
the castle of King Fisherman, and strong was
the defence at the entrance thereof.   Some of
the knights well knew that Perceval would
conquer him, for long since had it been prophesied that he who bare such shield should win
the Graal of him that sold God for money.

XXV

The knights saw Perceval coming and the
company of hermits with him right seemly to
behold, and much marvel had they thereof.
About a couple of bowshots above the bridge
was a chapel fashioned like the one at Camelot,
wherein was a sepulchre, and none knew who
lay therein. Perceval abideth thereby and his
company. He leaneth his shield and spear
against the chapel, and maketh fast his horse
and mule by the reins. He beholdeth the
sepulchre, that was right fair, and forthwith the
sepulchre openeth and the joinings fall apart and
the stone lifteth up in such wise that a man
might see the knight that lay within, of whom
came forth a smell of so sweet savour that it
seemed to the good men that were looking on
that it had been all embalmed. They found a
letter which testified that this knight was named
Josephus. So soon as the hermits beheld the
sepulchre open, they said to Perceval: 'Sir,
now at last know we well that you are the Good
Knight, the chaste, the holy.' The knights
that warded the bridge heard the tidings that
the sepulchre had opened at the coming of the
knight, whereof were they in the greater dismay, and well understood that it was he that
was first at the Graal. The tidings came to
the King that held the castle, and he bade his
knights not be dismayed for dread of a single
knight, for that he would have no force nor
power against them, nor might it never befall
but that one only of his own knights should be
enough to conquer him.

XXVI

Perceval was armed upon his horse. The hermits make the sign of the cross over him and bless him and commend him to God. And he holdeth his spear in rest and cometh toward the three knights that guard the first bridge. They all set upon him at once and break their spears upon his shield. One of them he smiteth with such force that he maketh him topple over into the river that runneth under the bridge, both him and his horse. Of him was he quit, for the river was wide and deep and swift. The others held out against him a much longer bout with sharp sword-play, but he vanquished them and smote them to pieces, and flung their bodies into the water. They of the second bridge came forward, that were right good knights, and many a tough bout had he of them and many a felon onslaught. Joseus that was his uncle's son was there, and said to the other hermits that right fainly would he go help him, but that he deemed it might be sin, and they bade him take no heed of that, for that great work of mercy would it be to destroy the enemies of Our Lord. He doeth off his grey cape and fettleth him in his frock, and taketh one of them that were doing battle with Perceval and trusseth him on his neck and so flingeth him into the river all armed, and Perceval slayeth the other twain and hurleth them into the river in like manner as the other.

XXVII

By the time he had won the two bridges he was full spent and weary, wherefore he bethinketh him of the lion, the manner whereof his uncle had told him. Then looketh he toward the entrance of the gateway and seeth the white lion, that stood upright on his two hinder feet, for that he was fain to see him. Perceval looketh him full between the two eyes, and understandeth that the lion is minded by the will of God to do him to wit that the knights of the third bridge are so hardy and of such strength that they may not be overcome of a single knight and our Lord God of his holy bounty open not the way, but that he must fain take the mule and carry the banner if he would conquer them. Perceval understandeth the white lion's intent, and giveth God thanks thereof and draweth him back, and Joseus the young man likewise. As soon as they look back, they see that the first bridge is already lifted up behind them.

XXVIII

Perceval cometh to where the white mule was, and she was starred on the forehead with a red cross. He mounteth thereupon, and taketh the banner and holdeth his sword drawn. So soon as the white lion seeth him coming, he unchaineth himself and runneth incontinent to the bridge that was lifted, right amidst the knights, and lowereth it forthwith. The King of Castle Mortal was on the battlements of the greater fortress of the castle, and crieth to the knights that warded the bridge, 'Lords,' saith he, 'You are the most chosen knights of my land and the hardiest, but no hardiment is it to lift the bridges on account of a single knight whom you durst not abide body to bodý, whereof meseemeth it great cowardize and not hardiment. But the lion is hardier than you all, that of his hardiment hath lowered the bridge. Wherefore now know I well that had I set him to ward the first bridge, he would have warded it better than these that have allowed themselves to be slain.'

XXIX

Thereupon, behold you Perceval come upon his white mule, sword drawn all naked in his fist, and cometh toward them of the third bridge, whereof he smiteth the first so sore that he overthroweth him into the water. Joseus the hermit cometh forward and would fain have seized the other twain, but they cry mercy of Perceval, and say that they will be at his will in all things, and so will believe on God and His sweet Mother and abandon their evil lord. And they of the fourth bridge say likewise. On such condition he alloweth them to live by the counsel of Joseus, and they cast away their arms and yield up the bridges at his will. Perceval thinketh within himself that God's virtue hath right great power, but that knight who hath force and power ought well to approve his prowess for God's sake. For of all that he shall do or suffer for Him, shall God be well pleased. For, were all the world against our Lord God, and He should grant to any single one that should be His champion all His power and might, he would conquer them all in one hour of the day. But He willeth that a man should travail for Him, even as He Himself suffered travail for His people.

XXX

Perceval cometh again back and alighteth of the white mule and delivereth the banner to Joseus, and then mounteth again on his destrier and cometh back to them of the fifth bridge, and these defend themselves right stoutly, for that hardy knights are they, and do battle against Perceval full sturdily. Joseus the hermit cometh thither and assaulteth them with passing great lustihood, that had the Lord God not saved him they would have overthrown and slain him. Howbeit, he holdeth the banner and grappleth them when he may lay hold, and grippeth them so strait that they may not help themselves. Perceval slayeth them and crusheth them and maketh them topple over into the water that ran swiftly beneath the bridge. When they of the sixth bridge saw that these were conquered, they cried mercy of Perceval and yielded themselves to him and delivered up their swords to him, and they of the seventh bridge likewise. When the red lion saw that the seventh bridge was won, and that the knights of the two bridges had yielded themselves up to Perceval, he leapt up with such fury that he burst his chain as had he been wood mad. He came to one of the knights and bit him and slew him,

whereof the white lion was full wroth, and **The**
runneth upon the other lion and teareth him to **lion**
pieces with his claws and teeth. **aideth well**

XXXI

Straightway thereafter he raiseth himself up
on his two hinder feet and looketh at Perceval,
and Perceval at him. Perceval understandeth
well the lion's intent, to wit, that they of the
last bridge are worse to conquer than the others,
and that they may not be conquered at all save
by the will of God and by him that is the lion.
And the lion warned him that he go not against
them with the banner, holy though it were, nor
receive them into mercy what surety soever
they might make, for that they are traitors, but
that he must fain mount upon the white mule,
for that she is a beast on God's side, and that
Joseus should bring the banner and all the
hermits go before, that are worshipful men
and of good life, so as to dismay the traitor
King, and so shall the end and the conquest of
the castle be brought nigh. Of all this the
lion made signs to Perceval, for speak he could
not. Great affiance hath Perceval in the lion's
warning. He alighteth of his destrier and
remounteth on the mule, and Joseus holdeth
the banner. The company of twelve hermits
was there, right seemly and holy. They draw
nigh the castle. The knights on the last bridge
see Perceval coming towards them and Joseus
the hermit holding the banner, by whom they
had seen their other fellows wrestled withal and
put to the worse.

XXXII

The virtue of Our Lord and the dignity of the banner and the goodness of the white mule and the holiness of the good hermits that made their orisons to Our Lord so struck the knights that they lost all power over themselves, but treason might not go forth of their hearts, wherefore right heavy were they of their kinsmen that they had seen slain before them. They bethought them that and if by mercy they might escape thence, they would never end until they had slain Perceval. They come to meet him and so cry him mercy passing sweetly in semblance, and say that they will do his will for ever and ever, so only he will let them depart safe and sound. Perceval looketh at the lion to know what he shall do; he seeth that the lion thinketh them traitors and disloyal, and that so they were destroyed and dead the King that was in the castle would have lost his force; and that, so Perceval will run upon them, the lion will help him slay them. Perceval telleth the knights that never will he have mercy upon them, and forthwith runneth upon them, sword drawn, and sorely it misliked him that they defended not themselves, insomuch that he all but left to slay them for that no defence found he in them. But the lion is so far from holding them in the like disdain, that he runneth upon them and biteth and slayeth them, and then casteth forth their limbs and bodies into the water. Perceval alloweth that this is well and seemly, and pleaseth him much of that he seeth the lion do, nor never before **The** had he seen any beast that he might love and **King** prize so highly as this one. **slayeth himself**

XXXIII

The King of Castle Mortal was on the battlements of the wall, and seeth how his knights are dead, and how the lion helpeth to slay the last. He setteth himself on the highest place of the walls, then lifteth the skirt of his habergeon and holdeth his sword all naked, that was right keen and well-tempered, and so smiteth himself right through the body, and falleth all adown the walls into the water, that was swift and deep, in such sort that Perceval saw him, and all the good hermits likewise, that marvelled much of a King that should slay himself in such manner; but they say according to the judgment of the scripture, that by right of evil man should the end be evil. On such wise was the end of this King of whom I tell you. Josephus relateth us how none ought to marvel that of three brothers, even though they be sons of the same father and mother, one brother should be evil; and the real marvel, saith he, is when one evil corrupteth not the two that are good, for that wickedness is so hard and keen and beguiling, and goodness so kindly and simple and humble. Cain and Abel were brothers-german, yet Cain slew his brother Abel, the one flesh betrayed the other. But great sorrow is it, saith Josephus, when the flesh that ought to be one becometh twain, and the one flesh goeth about by wickedness to deceive and

destroy the other. Josephus recordeth us by
this evil king that was so traitorous and false
and yet was of the lineage of the Good Soldier
Joseph of Abarimacie. This Joseph, as the
scripture witnesseth, was his uncle, and this
evil king was brother-german of King Fisherman, and brother of the good King Pelles that
had abandoned his land, in order that he might
serve God, and brother of the Widow Lady
that was Perceval's mother, the most loyal that
was ever in Great Britain. All these lineages
were in the service of Our Lord from the
beginning of their lives unto the end, save only
this evil King that perished so evilly as you
have heard.

XXXIV

You have heard how the King that had
seized the castle that had been King Fisherman's slew himself in such wise, and how his
knights were discomfited. Perceval entered
into the castle and the worshipful hermits
together with him. It seemed them when they
were come within into the master hall, that
they heard chant in an inner chapel *Gloria in
excelsis Deo*, and right sweet praising of Our
Lord. They found the halls right rich and
seemly and fairly adorned within. They found
the chapel open where the sacred hallows were
wont to be. The holy hermits entered therein
and made their orisons, and prayed the Saviour
of the World that He would swiftly restore to
them the most Holy Graal and the sacred
hallows that wont to be therewithin whereby
they might be comforted.

XXXV

The good men were there within with
Perceval, that much loved their company.
Josephus witnesseth us that the ancient knights
that were of the household of King Fisherman,
and the priests and damsels, departed so soon as
the King that slew himself had seized the castle,
for that they would not be at his court, and the
Lord God preserved them from him and made
them go into such a place as that they should be
in safety. The Saviour of the World well knew
that the Good Knight had won the castle by
his valour that should have been his own of
right, and sent back thither all them that had
served King Fisherman. Perceval made right
great joy of them when he saw them, and they
of him. They seemed well to be a folk that
had come from some place where God and His
commandments were honoured, and so indeed
had they.

XXXVI

The High History witnesseth us that when
the conquest of the castle was over, the Saviour
of the World was right joyous and well pleased
thereof. The Graal presented itself again in
the chapel, and the lance whereof the point
bleedeth, and the sword wherewith St. John
was beheaded that Messire Gawain won, and
the other holy relics whereof was right great
plenty. For our Lord God loved the place
much. The hermits went back to their
hermitages in the forest and served Our Lord

King Fisher-man his tomb as they had been wont. Joseus remained with Perceval at the castle as long as it pleased him, but the Good Knight searched out the land there where the New Law had been abandoned and its maintenance neglected. He reft the lives of them that would not maintain it and believe. The country was supported by him and made safe, and the Law of Our Lord exalted by his strength and valour. The priests and knights that repaired to the castle loved Perceval much, for, so far from his goodness minishing in ought, they saw from day to day how his valour and his faith in God increased and multiplied. And he showed them the sepulchre of his uncle King Fisherman in the chapel before the altar. The coffin was rich and the tabernacle costly and loaded of precious stones. And the priests and knights bear witness that as soon as the body was placed in the coffin and they were departed thence, they found on their return that it was covered by the tabernacle all dight as richly as it is now to be seen, nor might they know who had set it there save only the commandment of Our Lord And they say that every night was there a great brightness of light as of candles there, and they knew not whence it should come save of God. Perceval had won the castle by the command of God. The Graal was restored in the holy chapel, and the other hallows as you have heard. The evil believe was done away from the kingdom, and all were assured again in the New Law by the valour of the Good Knight.

BRANCH XIX

TITLE I

NOW is the story silent of Perceval and cometh back to King Arthur, the very matter thereof, like as testifieth the history, that in no place is corrupted and the Latin lie not. King Arthur was at Cardoil on one day of Whitsuntide that was right fair and clear, and many knights were in the hall. The King sate at meat and all the knights about him. The King looketh at the windows of the hall to right and left, and seeth that two sunbeams are shining within that fill the whole hall with light. Thereof he marvelleth much and sendeth without the hall to see what it might be. The messenger cometh back again and saith thereof that two suns appear to be shining, the one in the East and the other in the West. He marvelleth much thereat, and prayeth Our Lord that he may be permitted to know wherefore two suns should appear in such wise. A Voice appeared at one of the windows that said to him : ' King, marvel not hereof that two suns should appear in the sky, for our Lord God hath well the power, and know well that this is for joy of the conquest that the Good Knight hath made that took away the shield from herewithin. He hath won the land that be-

A longed to good King Fisherman from the evil damsel King of Castle Mortal, that did away thence with a the good believe, and therefore was it that the casket Graal was hidden. Now God so willeth that you go thither, and that you choose out the best knights of your court, for better pilgrimage may you never make, and what time you shall return hither, your faith shall be doubled and the people of Great Britain shall be better disposed and better taught to maintain the service of the Saviour.'

II

Thereupon the Voice departed, and well pleased was the King of that it had said. He sitteth at meat beside the Queen. Straightway behold you, a damsel that cometh of such beauty as never was greater, and clad right richly, and she beareth a coffer richer than ever you saw, for it was all of fine gold and set with precious stones that sparkled like fire. The coffer is not large. The damsel holdeth it between her hands. When she was alighted she cometh before the King and saluteth him the fairest she may and the Queen likewise. The King returneth her salute. 'Sir,' saith she, 'I am come to your court for that it is the sovran of all other, and so bring I you here this rich vessel that you see as a gift; and it hath within the head of a knight, but none may open the coffer save he alone that slew the knight. Wherefore I pray and beseech you, as you are the best king that liveth, that you first set your hand thereon, and in like manner afterwards make proof of your knights, and so the crime Trial and the blood-feud thereof be brought home to of the you or to any knight that may be within yonder. casket I pray you that the knight who shall be able to open the coffer wherein the head of the knight lieth, and who therefore is he that slew him, shall have grace of forty days after that you shall be returned from the Graal.' 'Damsel,' saith the King, 'How shall it be known who the knight was?' 'Sir,' saith she, 'Right eath, for the letters are sealed within that tell his name and the name of him that slew him.' The King granteth the damsel her will in such wise as she had asked of him. He hath received the coffer, then maketh her be set at meat and right richly honoured.

III

When the King had eaten, the damsel cometh before him. 'Sir,' saith she, 'Make your knights be summoned and ready for that which you have granted me, and you yourself first of all.' 'Damsel,' saith the King, 'Right willingly.' He setteth his hand to the coffer, thinking to open it, but it was not right that it should open for him. As he set his hand thereon the coffer sweated through just as had it been sprinkled all over and was wet with water. The King marvelled greatly, and so made Messire Gawain set his hand to it and Lancelot and all those of the court, but he that might open it was not among them. Messire Kay the Seneschal had served at meat. He heard say that the King and all the others had essayed and proved the

Kay boasteth himself coffer but might not open it. He is come thither, all uncalled for. 'Now, then, Kay,' saith the King, 'I had forgotten you.' 'By my head,' saith Kay, 'You ought not to forget me, for as good knight am I and of as much worth as they that you have called before me, and you ought not to have delayed to send for me. You have summoned all the others, and me not a whit, and yet am I as well able, or ought to be, to open the coffer as are they; for against as many knights have I defended me as they, and as many have I slain in defending my body as have they.' 'Kay,' saith the King, 'shall you be so merry and you may open the coffer, and if you have slain the knight whose head lieth therein? By my head, I that am King would fain that the coffer should not open for me, for never was no knight so poor as that he should have neither kinsman nor friend, for he is not loved of all the world that is hated by one man.' 'By my head,' saith Kay, 'I would that all the heads of all the knights I have slain, save one only, were in the midst of this hall, and that there were letters sealed with them to say that they were slain by me. Then would you believe what you are not willing to believe for the envious ones that think they are better worth than I, and yet have not served you so well.'

IV

'Kay,' saith the King, 'Come forward, there is no need of this.' Messire Kay the Seneschal cometh to the dais before the King, whereon was the coffer, and taketh it right

boldly and setteth one of his hands below it **The**
and the other above. The coffer opened as **casket**
soon as he clapped hand thereon, and the head **opened**
within could be seen all openly. A passing
delicate-savoured smell and right sweet issued
therefrom, so that not a knight in the hall
but smelt it. 'Sir,' saith Kay to the King,
'Now may you know that some prowess and
some hardiment have I done in your service,
nor might none of your knights that you prize
so highly open the coffer this day, nor would
you have known this day who is therein for
them! But now you know it by me, and therefore of so much ought you to be well pleased
with me!'

V

'Sir,' saith the damsel that had brought the
coffer, 'Let the letters be read that are within,
so shall you know who the knight was and of
what lineage, and what was the occasion of his
death.' The King sitteth beside the Queen,
and biddeth call one of his own chaplains.
Then maketh he all the knights in the hall be
seated and keep silence, and commandeth the
chaplain that he should spell out the letters of
gold all openly according as he should find them
written. The chaplain looketh at them, and
when he had scanned them down, began to sigh.
'Sir,' saith he to the King and Queen, 'hearken
to me, and all the other, your knights.

VI

'These letters say that the knight whose head
lieth in this vessel was named Lohot, and he

was son of King Arthur and Queen Guenievre.
He had slain on a day that is past, Logrin the
Giant, by his hardiment. Messire Kay the
Seneschal was passing by there, and so found
Lohot sleeping upon Logrin, for such was his
custom that he went to sleep upon the man after
that he had slain him. Messire Kay smote off
Lohot's head, and so left the head and the body
on the piece of ground. He took the head of
the Giant and so bore it to the court of King
Arthur. He gave the King and Queen and all
the barons of the court to understand that he
had slain him, but this did he not; rather, that
he did was to slay Lohot, according to the
writing and the witness of these letters.' When
the Queen heareth these letters and this witting
of her son that came thus by his death, she
falleth in a swoon on the coffer. After that
she taketh the head between her two hands, and
knew well that it was he by a scar that he had
on his face when he was a child. The King
himself maketh dole thereof so sore that none
may comfort him, for before these tidings he
had thought that his son was still on live and
that he was the Best Knight in the world, and
when the news came to his court that the Knight
of the Golden Circlet had slain the Knight of
the Dragon, he supposed that it had been Lohot
his son, for that none had named Perceval nor
Gawain nor Lancelot. And all they of the
court are right sorrowful for the death of
Lohot, and Messire Kay hath departed, and
if the damsel had not respited the day until the
fortieth after the King's return, vengeance would

have been taken of Kay or ever he might have turned him thence. For never did no man see greater dole made in the King's court than they of the Table Round made for the youth. King Arthur and the Queen were so stricken of sorrow that none durst call upon them to make cheer. The damsel that brought thither the coffer was well avenged of the shame that Messire Kay the Seneschal had done her on a day that was past, for this thing would not have been known so soon save it had been by her.

Arthur goeth on pilgrimage

VII

When the mourning for the King's son was abated, Lancelot and many others said to him, 'Sir, you know well that God willeth you should go to the castle that was King Fisherman's on pilgrimage to the most Holy Graal, for it is not right to delay a thing that one hath in covenant with God.' 'Lords,' saith the King, 'right willingly will I go, and thereto am I right well disposed.' The King apparelleth himself for the pilgrimage, and saith that Messire Gawain and Lancelot shall go with him, without more knights, and taketh a squire to wait upon his body, and the Queen herself would he have taken thither but for the mourning she made for her son, whereof none might give her any comfort. But or ever the King departed he made the head be brought into the Isle of Avalon, to a chapel of Our Lady that was there, where was a worshipful holy hermit that was well loved of Our Lord.

Kay fleeth to Briant The King departed from Cardoil and took leave of the Queen and all the knights. Lancelot and Messire Gawain go along with him and a squire that carrieth their arms. Kay the Seneschal was departed from the court for dread of the King and his knights. He durst not abide in the Greater Britain, and so betook him into the Lesser. Briant of the Isles was of great power in these times, a knight of great strength and hardiment, for all Great Britain had had many disputes between him and King Arthur. His land was full strong of castles and forests and right fruitful, and many good knights had he in his land. When he knew that Kay the Seneschal had departed in such sort from the court, and that he had crossed the sea, he sent for him and held him of his household, and said that he would hold him harmless against the King and against all men. When he knew that the King had departed he began to war upon the land and to slay his men and to challenge his castles.

BRANCH XX

TITLE I

THE story saith that King Arthur goeth his way and Lancelot and Messire Gawain with him, and they had ridden so far one day that night came on in a forest and they might find no hold. Messire Gawain marvelled him much that they had ridden the day long without finding neither hold nor hermitage. Night was come and the sky was dark and the forest full of gloom. They knew not whitherward to turn to pass the night. 'Lords,' saith the King, 'Where may we be able to alight to-night?' 'Sir, we know not, for this forest is right wearisome.' They make the squire climb up a tall tree and tell him to look as far as he may to try whether he may espy any hold or house where they may lodge. The squire looketh on all sides, and then telleth them he seeth a fire a long way off as if it were in a waste house, but that he seeth nought there save the fire and the house. 'Take good heed,' saith Lancelot, 'in which quarter it is, so that you may know well how to lead us thither.' He saith that right eath may he lead them.

II

With that he cometh down and mounteth again on his hackney, and they go forward a great pace and ride until they espy the fire

and the hold.   They pass on over a bridge of
wattles, and find the courtyard all deserted and
the house from within great and high and
hideous.   But there was a great fire within
whereof the heat might be felt from afar.   They
alight of their horses, and the squire draweth
them on one side amidst the hall, and the
knights set them beside the fire all armed.
The squire seeth a chamber in the house and
entereth thereinto to see if he may find any
meat for the horses, but he cometh forth again
the swiftest he may and crieth right sweetly on
the Mother of the Saviour.   They ask him
what aileth him, and he saith that he hath found
the most treacherous chamber ever he found
yet, for he felt there, what with heads and
what with hands, more than two hundred men
dead, and saith that never yet felt he so sore
afeared.   Lancelot went into the chamber to
see whether he spake true, and felt the men
that lay dead, and groped among them from
head to head and felt that there was a great
heap of them there, and came back and sate
at the fire all laughing.   The King asketh
whether the squire had told truth.   Lancelot
answereth him yea, and that never yet had he
found so many dead men together.   'Methinketh,' saith Messire Gawain, 'Sith that
they are dead we have nought to fear of them,
but God protect us from the living.'

III

While they were talking thus, behold you a
damsel that cometh into the dwelling on foot

and all alone, and she cometh lamenting right The grievously. 'Ha, God!' saith she, 'How Damsel long a penance is this for me, and when will of the it come to an end?' She seeth the knights Beards sitting in the midst of the house. 'Fair Lord God,' saith she, 'Is he there within through whom I am to escape from this great dolour?' The knights hearken to her with great wonderment. They look and see her enter within the door, and her kirtle was all torn with thorns and briars in the forest. Her feet were all bleeding for that she was unshod. She had a face of exceeding great beauty. She carried the half of a dead man, and cast it into the chamber with the others. She knew Lancelot again so soon as she saw him. 'Ha, God!' saith she, 'I am quit of my penance! Sir,' saith she, 'Welcome may you be, you and your company!' Lancelot looketh at her in wonderment. 'Damsel,' saith he, 'Are you a thing on God's behalf?' 'Certes, Sir,' saith she, 'Yea! nor be you adread of nought! I am the Damsel of the Castle of Beards, that was wont to deal with knights so passing foully as you have seen. You did away the toll that was levied on the knights that passed by, and you lay in the castle that demanded it of them that passed through the demesne thereof. But you had me in covenant that so the Holy Graal should appear to you, you would come back to me, for otherwise never should I have been willing to let you go. You returned not, for that you saw not the Graal. For the shame that I did to knights was this penance laid upon

A foul me in this forest and this manor, to last until
penance such time as you should come. For the cruelty
I did them was sore grievous, for never was
knight brought to me but I made his nose be
cut off or his eyes thrust out, and some were
there as you saw that had their feet or their
hands stricken off. Now have I paid full dear
thereof since, for needs must I carry into this
chamber all the knights that are slain in this
forest, and within this manor must I cast them
according to the custom thereof, alone, without
company; and this knight that I carried in but
now hath lain so long in the forest that wild
beasts have eaten the half of his body. Now
am I quit of this foul penance, thanks to God
and to you, save only that I must go back when
it shall be daylight in like manner as I came
here.'

IV

'Damsel,' saith Lancelot, 'Right glad am I
that we should have come to lodge the night
here within, for love of you, for never saw I
damsel that might do so cruel penance.' 'Sir,'
saith she, 'You know not yet what it is, but
you will know it ere long this night, both you
and your fellows, and the Lord God shield
you from death and from mischief! Every
night cometh a rout of knights that are black
and foul and hideous, albeit none knoweth whence
they come, and they do battle right sore the
one against other, and the stour endureth of a
right long while; but one knight that came
within yonder by chance, the first night I came

hither, in like manner as you have come, made **The**
a circle round me with his sword, and I sate **knights'**
within it, as soon as I saw them coming, and so **ghosts**
had I no dread of them, for I had in remembrance
the Saviour of the World and His passing sweet
Mother.   And you will do the same, and you
believe me herein, for these are knights fiends.'
Lancelot draweth his sword and maketh a
great circle round the house-place, and they
were within.

V

Thereupon, behold you the knights that come
through the forest with such a rushing as it
seemed they would rend it all up by the roots.
Afterward, they enter into the manor and
snatch great blazing firebrands and fling them
one at another.   They enter into the house
battling together, and are keen to fall upon the
knights, but they may not.   They hurl the firebrands at them from afar, but they are holding
their shields and their swords naked.   Lancelot maketh semblant as though he would leap
towards them, and sore great cowardize it
seemeth him not to go against them.   'Sir,'
saith the damsel, 'Take heed that you go not
forth of the circle, for you will be in sore
jeopardy of death, for well you see what evil
folk be these.'   Lancelot was not minded to
hold himself back, but that he would go toward
them sword drawn, and they run upon him on
all sides, but he defendeth him stoutly and
smiteth the burning firebrands so that he maketh
red-hot charcoal fly, and thrusteth his sword

amidst their faces. King Arthur and Messire Gawain leap up to help Lancelot and smite upon these evil folk and cut them limb from limb, and they bellow like fiends so that the whole forest resoundeth thereof. And when they fell to the ground, they may no longer endure, but become fiends and ashes, and their bodies and their horses become devils all black in the shape of ravens that come forth of their bodies. They marvel right sore what this may be, and say that such hostel is right grievous.

VI

When they had put them all to the worse, they sate them down again and rested; but scarce were they seated or ever another rout of yet blacker folk came about them, and they bare spears burning and flaming, and many of them carried dead knights that they had slain in the forest, and dropped them in the midst of the house, and then bid the damsel carry and set them with the others. Howbeit, she answereth that she is quit of their commandment and service, nor no longer is forced to do nought for them sith that she hath done her penance. They thrust forward their spears toward the King and the two knights, as though they were come to avenge their companions; but they all three leapt up together and attacked them right stoutly. But this rout was greater and of knights more hideous. They began to press the King and his knights hard, and they might not put them to the worse as they did the others. And while they were thus in the

thickest of the conflict, they heard the stroke **A bell**
of a bell sounding, and forthwith the knight **soundeth**
fiends departed and hurried away a great pace.
'Lords,' saith the damsel, 'Had this sound not
been heard, scarce might you have endured, for
yet another huge rout of this folk was coming
in such sort as that none might have withstood
them, and this sound have I heard every night,
whereby my life hath been saved.'

VII

Josephus telleth us that as at this time was
there no bell neither in Greater Britain nor in
Lesser; but folk were called together by a
horn, and in many places there were sheets of
steel, and in other places clappers of wood.
King Arthur marvelled him much of this
sound, so clear and sweet was it, and it well
seemed him that it came on God's behalf,
and right fain was he to see a bell and so
he might. They were the night until the
morrow in the house, as I tell you. The
damsel took leave of them and so departed.
As they came forth of the hold, they met three
hermits that told them they were going to
search for the bodies that were in this manor so
that they might bury them in a waste chapel
that was hard by, for such knights had lain
there as that henceforward the haunting of the
evil folk would be stayed in such sort as that
they would have no more power to do hurt to
any, wherefore they would set therewithin a
worshipful hermit that should build up the place
in holiness for the service of God. The King

The knight married was right joyful thereof, and told them that it had been too perilous. They parted from the hermits and entered into a forest, nor was there never a day so long as King Arthur was on pilgrimage, so saith the history, but he heard the sound of one single bell every hour, whereof he was right glad. He bade Messire Gawain and Lancelot that they should everywhere conceal his name, and that they should call him not Lord but Comrade. They yielded him his will, and prayed to Our Lord that He would guide and lead them to such a castle and such a hostel as that they might be lodged honourably therein. They rode on until evening drew nigh, and they found a right fair hold in the forest, whereinto they entered and alighted. The damsel of the hold came to meet them and made them right great cheer, then made them be disarmed, afterward bringeth them right rich robes to wear. She looketh at Lancelot and knoweth him again.

VIII

'Sir,' saith she, 'You had once, on a day that is past, right great pity of me, and saved me my honour, whereof am I in great unhappiness. But better love I to suffer misease in honour, than to have plenty and abundance in shame or reproach, for shame endureth, but sorrow is soon overpassed.' Thereupon behold you the knight of the hold, whither he cometh from shooting in the forest and maketh carry in full great plenty venison of deer and wild boar. He alighted to greet the knights, and began to

laugh when he saw Lancelot. 'By my head,' against
saith he, 'I know you well. For you dis- his will
appointed me of the thing I best loved in the
world, and made me marry this damsel that
never yet had joy of me, nor never shall have.'
'Fair Sir,' saith Lancelot, 'You will do your
pleasure therein, for she is yours. Truth it is
that I made you marry her, for you were fain
to do her a disgrace and a shame in such sort
that her kinsfolk would have had shame of her.'
'By my head,' saith the knight, 'the damsel
that I loved before loveth you no better hereof,
nay, rather, fain would she procure your vexa-
tion and your hurt and your shame if she may,
and great power hath she in this forest.' 'Sir,'
saith Lancelot, 'I have sithence spoken to her
and she to me, and so hath she told me her will
and her wish.' Thereupon the knight bade the
knights take water, and the lady taketh the basins
and presenteth water to the knights. 'Avoid,
damsel,' saith the King, 'Take it away! Never,
please God, shall it befall that we should accept
such service from you.' 'By my head,' saith
the knight, 'But so must you needs do, for
other than she shall not serve you to-night in
this matter, or otherwise shall you not eat with
me this night there within.'

IX

Lancelot understandeth that the knight is not
overburdened of courtesy, and he seeth the
table garnished of good meat, and bethinketh
him he will not do well to lose such ease, for
misease enough had they the night before.

He maketh the King take water of the lady, and the same service did she for all of them. The knight biddeth them be seated. The King would have made the lady sit beside him at the table, but the Knight said that there she should not sit. She goeth to sit among the squires as she was wont to do. The knights are sorry enough thereof, but they durst not gainsay the will of her lord. When they had eaten, the knight said to Lancelot, 'Now may you see what she hath gained of me by your making me take her perforce; nor never, so help me God, so long as I live shall she be honoured otherwise by me, for so have I promised her that I love far more.' 'Sir,' saith Lancelot, 'To my thinking, you do ill herein and a sin, and meseemeth you should have great blame thereof of them that know it, and may your churlishness be your own, for nought thereof take I to myself.'

x

Lancelot telleth the King and Messire Gawain that were he not lodged in his hostel, and had him outside of the hold, he would willingly have set the blood of his body on it but he would have handled him in such sort as that the lady should be maintained in greater honour, either by force or by prayer, in like manner as he did when he made him marry her. They were right well lodged the night and lay in the hold until the morrow, when they departed thence, and rode right busily on their journeys until they came into a very different land, scarce inhabited of any folk, and found a little castle in a combe. They came thitherward and saw that the enclosure of the castle was fallen down into an abysm, so that none might approach it on that side, but it had a right fair gateway and a door tall and wide whereby one entered. They beheld a chapel that was right fair and rich, and below was a great ancient hall. They saw a priest appear in the midst of the castle, bald and old, that had come forth of the chapel. They are come thither and alighted, and asked the priest what the castle was, and he told them that it was the great Tintagel. 'And how is this ground all caved in about the castle?' 'Sir,' saith the priest, 'I will tell you. Sir,' saith he, 'King Uther Pendragon, that was father of King Arthur, held a great court and summoned all his barons. The King of this castle that then was here was named Gorlois. He went to the court and took his wife with him, that was named Ygerne, and she was the fairest dame in any kingdom. King Uther sought acquaintance of her for her great beauty, and regarded her and honoured her more than all the others of his court. King Gorlois departed thence and made the Queen come back to this castle for the dread that he had of King Uther Pendragon. King Uther was very wroth with him, and commanded him to send back the Queen his wife. King Gorlois said that he would not. Thereupon King Uther Pendragon defied him, and then laid siege about this castle where the Queen was. King Gorlois was gone to seek for succour. King Uther Pendragon

Merlin had Merlin with him of whom you have heard
his grave tell, that was so crafty.   He made him be
changed into the semblance of King Gorlois, so
that he entered there within by Merlin's art and
lay that night with the Queen, and so begat
King Arthur in a great hall that was next to
the enclosure there where this abysm is.   And
for this sin hath the ground sunken in on this
wise.'   He cometh with them toward the
chapel that was right fair, and had a right rich
sepulchre therein.   'Lords, in this sepulchre
was placed the body of Merlin, but never
mought it be set inside the chapel, wherefore
perforce it remained outside.   And know of a
very truth that the body lieth not within the
sepulchre, for, so soon as it was set therein, it
was taken out and snatched away, either on
God's behalf or the Enemy's, but which we
know not.'

XI

'Sir,' saith King Arthur, 'And what became
of King Gorlois!'   'Sir,' saith he, 'The
King slew him on the morrow of the night he
lay with his wife, and so forthwith espoused
Queen Ygerne, and in such manner as I tell you
was King Arthur conceived in sin that is now
the best King in the world.'   King Arthur hath
heard this as concerning his birth that he knew
not, and is a little shamed thereof and con-
founded on account of Messire Gawain and
Lancelot.   He himself marvelleth much thereof,
and much it misliketh him that the priest hath
said so much.   They lay the night in the hold,

and so departed thence on the morrow when **Of things** they had heard mass. Lancelot and Messire **changed** Gawain, that thought they knew the forest, found the land so changed and different that they knew not whither they were become, and such an one as should come into the land that had been King Fisherman's, and he should come again another time within forty days, should not find the castle within a year.

XII

Josephus telleth us that the semblances of the islands changed themselves by reason of the divers adventures that by the pleasure of God befell therein, and that the quest of adventures would not have pleased the knights so well and they had not found them so different. For, when they had entered into a forest or an island where they had found any adventure, and they came there another time, they found holds and castles and adventures of another kind, so that their toils and travails might not weary them, and also for that God would that the land should be conformed to the New Law. And they were the knights that had more toil and travail in seeking adventures than all the knights of the world before them, and in holding to that whereof they had made covenant; nor of no court of no king in the world went forth so many good knights as went forth from the court of King Arthur, and but that God loved them so much, never might they have endured such toil and travail as they did from day to day; for without fail, good knights were they, and good

Lancelot knights not only to deal hard buffets, but rather
his in that they were loyal and true, and had faith
covenant in the Saviour of the World and His sweet
Mother, and therefore dreaded shame and loved
honour. King Arthur goeth on his way and
Messire Gawain and Lancelot with him, and
they pass through many strange countries, and
so enter into a great forest. Lancelot called to
remembrance the knight that he had slain in the
Waste City whither behoved him to go, and knew
well that the day whereon he should come was
drawing nigh. He told King Arthur as much,
and then said, that and he should go not, he
would belie his covenant. They rode until
they came to a cross where the ways forked.
'Sir,' saith Lancelot, 'Behoveth me go to acquit
me of my pledge, and I go in great adventure
and peril of death, nor know I whether I may
live at all thereafter, for I slew the knight, albeit
I was right sorry thereof, but or ever I slew
him, I had to swear that I would go set my
head in the like jeopardy as he had set his.
Now the day draweth nigh that I must go
thither, for I am unwilling to fail of my
covenant, whereof I should be blamed, and, so
God grant me to escape therefrom, I will follow
you speedily.' The King embraceth him and
kisseth him at parting and Messire Gawain
also, and they pray God preserve his body
and his life, and that they may see him
again ere it be long. Lancelot would willingly
have sent salute to the Queen had he durst, for
she lay nearer his heart than aught beside, but
he would not that the King nor Messire Gawain

should misdeem of the love they might carry to their kinswoman. The love is so rooted in his heart that he may not leave it, into what peril soever he may go; rather, he prayeth God every day as sweetly as he may, that He save the Queen, and that he may deliver his body from this jeopardy. He hath ridden until that he cometh at the hour of noon into the Waste City, and findeth the city empty as it was the first time he was there.

XIII

In the city wherein Lancelot had arrived were many waste houses and rich palaces fallen down. He had scarce entered within the city when he heard a great cry and lamentation of dames and damsels, but he knew not on which side it was, and they say: 'Ha, God, how hath the knight betrayed us that slew the knight, inasmuch as he returneth not! This day is the day come that he ought to redeem his pledge! Never again ought any to put trust in knight, for that he cometh not! The others that came hither before him have failed us, and so will he also for dread of death; for he smote off the head of the comeliest knight that was in this kingdom and the best, wherefore ought he also to have his own smitten off, but good heed taketh he to save it if he may!' Thus spake the damsels. Lancelot much marvelled where they might be, for nought could he espy of them, albeit he cometh before the palace, there where he slew the knight. He alighteth, then maketh fast his horse's reins to a ring that was

Lancelot fixed in the mounting-stage of marble. Scarce
prayeth hath he done so, when a knight alighteth, tall
and comely and strong and deliver, and he was
clad in a short close-fitted jerkin of silk, and
held the axe in his hand wherewith Lancelot
had smitten off the head of the other knight,
and he came sharpening it on a whet-stone to
cut the better. Lancelot asketh him, 'What
will you do with this axe?' 'By my head,'
saith the knight, 'That shall you know in such
sort as my brother knew when you cut off his
head, so I may speed of my business.' 'How?'
saith Lancelot, 'Will you slay me then?'
'That shall you know,' saith he, 'or ever you
depart hence. Have you not loyally promised
hereof that you would set your head in the same
jeopardy as the knight set his, whom you slew
without defence? And no otherwise may you
depart therefrom. Wherefore now come forward without delay and kneel down and stretch
your neck even as my brother did, and so will
I smite off your head, and, if you do not this
of your own good will, you shall soon find one
that shall make you do it perforce, were you
twenty knights as good as you are one. But
well I know that you have not come hither for
this, but only to fulfil your pledge, and that
you will raise no contention herein.' Lancelot
thinketh to die, and is minded to abide by that
he hath in covenant without fail, wherefore he
lieth down on the ground as it were on a cross,
and crieth mercy of God. He mindeth him
of the Queen, and crieth God of mercy and
saith, 'Ha, Lady,' saith he, 'Never shall I see

you more! but, might I have seen you yet once **Lancelot**
again before I die, exceeding great comfort had **loveth**
it been to me, and my soul would have departed **well**
from me more at ease. But this, that never
shall I see you more, as now it seemeth me,
troubleth me more than the death whereby
behoveth me to die, for die one must when one
hath lived enough long. But faithfully do I
promise you that my love shall fail you not yet,
and never shall it be but that my soul shall love
you in the other world like as my body hath
loved you in this, if thus the soul may love!'
With that the tears fell from his eyes, nor,
never sithence that he was knight, saith the
story, had he wept for nought that had befallen
him nor for heaviness of heart, but this time
and one other. He taketh three blades of
grass and so eateth thereof in token of the holy
communion, then signeth him of the cross and
blesseth him, riseth up, setteth himself on his
knees and stretcheth forth his neck. The
knight lifteth up the axe. Lancelot heareth
the blow coming, boweth his head and the axe
misseth him. He saith to him, 'Sir Knight,
so did not my brother that you slew; rather,
he held his head and neck quite still, and so
behoveth you to do!' Two damsels appeared
at the palace-windows of passing great beauty,
and they knew Lancelot well. So, as the
knight was aiming a second blow, one of the
damsels crieth to him, 'And you would have
my love for evermore, throw down the axe and
cry the knight quit! Otherwise have you lost
me for ever!' The knight forthwith flingeth

down the axe and falleth at Lancelot's feet and crieth mercy of him as of the most loyal knight in the world. 'But you? Have mercy on me, you! and slay me not!' saith Lancelot, 'For it is of you that I ought to pray mercy!' 'Sir,' saith the knight, 'Of a surety will I not do this! Rather will I help you to my power to save your life against all men, for all you have slain my brother.' The damsels come down from the palace and are come to Lancelot.

XIV

'Sir,' say they to Lancelot, 'Greatly ought we to love you, yea, better than all knights in the world beside. For we are the two damsels, sisters, that you saw so poor at the Waste Castle where you lay in our brother's house. You and Messire Gawain and another knight gave us the treasure and the hold of the robber-knights that you slew; for this city which is waste and the Waste Castle of my brother would never again be peopled of folk, nor should we never have had the land again, save a knight had come hither as loyal as are you. Full a score knights have arrived here by chance in the same manner as you came, and not one of them but hath slain a brother or a kinsman and cut off his head as you did to the knight, and each one promised to return at the day appointed; but all failed of their covenant, for not one of them durst come to the day; and so you had failed us in like manner as the others, we should have lost this city without recovery and the castles that are its appanages.'

XV

So the knight and the damsels lead Lancelot into the palace and then make him be disarmed. They hear presently how the greatest joy in the world is being made in many parts of the forest, that was nigh the city. 'Sir,' say the damsels, 'Now may you hear the joy that is made of your coming. These are the burgesses and dwellers in the city that already know the tidings.' Lancelot leaneth at the windows of the hall, and seeth the city peopled of the fairest folk in the world, and great thronging in the broad streets and the great palace, and clerks and priests coming in long procession praising God and blessing Him for that they may now return to their church, and giving benison to the knight through whom they are free to repair thither. Lancelot was much honoured throughout the city. The two damsels are at great pains to wait upon him, and right great worship had he of all them that were therewithin and them that came thither, both clerks and priests.

Assembly
of tourney

THEREWITHAL the history is silent of Lancelot, and speaketh word of the King and Messire Gawain, that are in sore misgiving as concerning him, for right gladly would they have heard tidings of him. They met a knight that was coming all armed, and Messire Gawain asketh him whence he came, and he said that he came from the land of the Queen of the Golden Circlet, to whom a sore loss hath befallen; for the Son of the Widow Lady had won the Circlet of Gold for that he had slain the Knight of the Dragon, and she was to keep it safe for him and deliver it up to him at his will. 'But now hath Nabigant of the Rock reft her thereof, and a right outrageous knight is he and puissant; wherefore hath he commanded a damsel that she bring it to an assembly of knights that is to be held in the Meadow of the Tent of the two damsels, there where Messire Gawain did away the evil custom. The damsel that will bring the Golden Circlet will give it to the knight that shall do best at the assembly. Nabigant is keenly set upon having it, and maketh the more sure for that once aforetime he hath had it by force of arms. And I am going to the knights that

84

know not these tidings, in order that when they
shall hear them, they shall go to the assembly.'
Therewithal the knight departeth. The King
and Messire Gawain have ridden so far that they
come to the tent where Messire Gawain destroyed
the evil custom by slaying the two knights. He
found the tent garnished within and without in like
manner as it was when he was there, and Messire
Gawain made the King be seated on a quilted
mattress of straw, right costly, and thereafter be
disarmed of a squire, and he himself disarmed him,
and they washed their hands and faces for the
rust wherewith both of them were besmuttered.
And Messire Gawain found the chests un-
locked that were at the head of the couch,
and made the King be apparelled of white rich
stuffs that he found, and a robe of cloth of silk
and gold, and he clad himself in the like manner,
neither was the chest not a whit disfurnished
thereby, for the tent was all garnished of rich
adornments. When they were thus dight, a
man might have sought far or ever he should
find so comely knights.

II

Thereupon, behold you the two Damsels of
the Tent coming. 'Damsels,' saith Messire
Gawain, 'Welcome may you be.' 'Sir,' say
they, 'Good adventure may you have both
twain. It seemeth us that you take right boldly
that which is ours, yet never for neither of us
would you do a thing whereof you were be-
seeched.' 'Messire Gawain,' saith the elder,
'No knight is there in this kingdom but would

be right joyous and he supposed that I loved him, and I prayed you of your love on a day that is past, for the valour of your knighthood, yet never did you grant it me.   How durst you have affiance in me of aught, and take the things that are mine own so boldly, when I may not have affiance in you?'   'Damsel, for your courtesy and the good custom of the land; for you told me when the evil customs were overthrown, that all the honours and all the courtesies that are due to knights should ever be ready within for all them that should come hither for harbour.'   'Messire Gawain, you say true, but of right might one let the courtesy tarry and pay back churlishness by churlishness.

III

'The assembly of knights will begin to-morrow in this launde that is so fair.   There will be knights in plenty, and the prize will be the Circlet of Gold.   Now shall we see who will do best.   The assembly will last three whole days, and of one thing at least you may well make boast between you and your comrade, that you have the fairest hostel and the most pleasant and the most quiet of any knights at the assembly.'   The younger damsel looketh at King Arthur.   'And you,' saith she, 'What will you do?   Will you be as strange toward us as Messire Gawain is friendly with others?'

IV

'Damsel,' saith the King, 'Messire Gawain will do his pleasure and I mine.   Strange shall

I not be in respect of you, nor toward other at the
damsels; rather shall they be honoured on my Tent
part so long as I live, and I myself will be
at your commandment.' 'Sir,' saith she,
'Gramercy greatly. I pray you, therefore, that
you be my knight at the tournament.' 'Damsel,
this ought I not to refuse you, and right glad at
heart shall I be and I may do aught that shall
please you; for all knights ought to be at pains
for the sake of dame or damsel.' 'Sir,' saith
she, 'What is your name?'

V

'Damsel,' saith he, 'My name is Arthur,
and I am of Tincardoil.' 'Have you nought
to do with King Arthur?' 'Damsel, already
have I been many times at his court, and, if he
loved me not nor I him, I should not be in
Messire Gawain's company. In truth, he is
the King in the world that I love best.' The
damsel looketh at King Arthur, but wotteth not
a whit that it is he, and full well is she pleased
with the seeming and countenance of him. As
for the King, lightly might he have trusted that
he should have her as his lady-love so long
as he remained with her; but there is much to
say between his semblant and his thought, for he
showeth good semblant toward the damsel, that
hath over much affiance therein, but his thought
is on Queen Guenievre in what place soever he
may be. For nought loveth he so well as her.

VI

The damsels made stable the horses and
purvey for the bodies of the knights right richly

The at night, and they lay in two right rich beds in
damsels the midst of the hall, and their arms were all set
ready before. The damsels would not depart
until such time as they were asleep. The
harness of the knights that came to the assembly
came on the morrow from all parts. They set
up their booths and stretched their tents all
round about the launde of the forest. King
Arthur and Messire Gawain were risen in the
morning and saw the knights come from all
parts. The elder damsel cometh to Messire
Gawain and saith to him, 'Sir,' saith she, 'I
will that you bear to-day red arms that I will
lend you, for the love of me, and take heed that
they be well employed, and I desire that you
should not be known by your arms; rather let
it be said that you are the Red Knight, and you
shall allow it accordingly.' 'Damsel, Gramercy
greatly!' saith Messire Gawain, 'I will do my
endeavour in arms the best I may for love of
you.' The younger damsel cometh to King
Arthur; 'Sir,' saith she, 'My sister hath made
her gift and I will make mine. I have a suit
of arms of old, the richest that knight may
wear, that I will lend you, for methinketh they
will be better employed on you than on ever
another knight; so I pray you that you remember me at the assembly in like manner as
I shall ofttimes remember you.'

VII

'Damsel,' saith the King, 'Gramercy! No
knight is there that should see you but ought to
have you in remembrance in his heart for your

courtesy and your worth.' The knights were and their knights come about the tents. The King and Messire Gawain were armed and had made caparison their horses right ·richly. The damsel that should give the Golden Circlet was come. Nabigant of the Rock had brought great fellowships of knights together with him, and ordinance was made for the assembly.

VIII

The younger damsel saith to King Arthur: 'Well may you know that no knight that is here this day hath better arms than are yours, wherefore take heed that you show you to be good knight for love of me.' 'Damsel,' saith King Arthur, 'God grant that I be so.' So they laid hold on their reins and mounted their horses, that made great leaping and went away a great gallop. Saith the younger damsel to her sister: 'What think you of my knight, doth he not please you?' 'Yea,' saith the elder, 'But sore misliketh me of Messire Gawain for that he is not minded to do as I would have him. But he shall yet aby it dear.' King Arthur and Messire Gawain strike into the midst of the assembly like as it were two lions unchained, and at their first coming they smite down two knights to the ground under the feet of their horses. Messire Gawain taketh the two horses and sendeth them by a squire to the Damsels of the Tent, that made much joy thereof. After that were they not minded to take more booty as of horses or arms, but searched the fellowships on one side and the other; nor was there

no knight that came against them but they
pierced his shield or bore him to the ground,
insomuch as none was there that might endure
their buffets. Nabigant espieth Messire Gawain
and cometh toward him, and Messire Gawain
toward him again, and they hurtle together
either on other so strongly that Messire Gawain
beareth Nabigant to the ground, him and his
horse together all in a heap. And King
Arthur was not idle, for no knight durst come
against him but he overthrew him, so as that all
withdrew them back and avoided his buffets.
And many knights did well that day at the
assembly, but none might be the match of either
of them twain in deeds of arms, for, save it
were Lancelot or Perceval, were no knights on
live that had in them so much hardiment and
valour. After that it was evensong the knights
drew them back to their tents, and they say all
that the Knight of the Golden Arms and the
Knight of the Red Arms had done better than
they all at the assembly. King Arthur and
Messire Gawain come back to the tent of the
damsels, that make disarm them and do upon
them the rich robes and make great joy of
them. Thereupon, behold you, a dwarf that
cometh: 'Damsels, make great joy! for all
they of the assembly say with one accord that
your knights have done best this day.' King
Arthur and Messire Gawain sate to eat, and
right well were they served of every kind of
meats and of great cups of wine and sops in
wine. King Arthur made the younger damsel
sit beside him, and Messire Gawain the elder in

like manner, and when they had eaten they went **Gawain's**
to lie down and fell on sleep, for right sore **ill**
weary were they and forspent of the many **covenant**
buffets they had given and received, and they
slept until the morrow.

IX

When the day appeared they rose up. Thereupon, behold you the younger damsel where
she cometh and saluteth King Arthur. 'And
you, damsel!' saith King Arthur, 'God give
you joy and good adventure!' 'Sir,' saith
she, 'I will that you bear to-day these white
arms that you see here, and that you do no
worse to-day than yesterday you did, sith that
better you may not do.' 'Messire Gawain,'
saith the elder damsel, 'Remember you of the
King there where his land was compassed
about of a wall of stone, and you harboured
one night in his castle, what time you went to
seek for the sword wherewith John Baptist
was beheaded, when he was fain to take away
the sword from you, whereof you had so sore
misliking? Natheless, he yielded you up the
sword upon covenant that you should do that
which a damsel should first ask you to do
thereafter, and you promised him loyally that
so would you do?' 'Certes, damsel,' saith
Messire Gawain, 'Well do I remember the
same.' 'Now, therefore,' saith the damsel,
'would I fain prove whether you be indeed
so loyal as men say, and whether you will
hold your covenant that you made. Wherefore
I pray and beseech you that this day you shall

be he that doth worst of all the knights at the assembly, and that you bear none other arms save your own only, so as that you shall be known again of all them that are there present. And, so you will not do this, then will you have failed of your covenant, and I myself will go tell the King that you have broken the promise that you made to him right loyally.' 'Damsel,' saith Messire Gawain, 'Never yet brake I covenant with none, so it were such as I might fulfil or another on my behalf.' King Arthur made arm him of the white arms that the younger damsel had given him, and Messire Gawain of his own, but sore it irked him of this that the damsel hath laid upon him to do, sith that needs must he lose worship and he hold to his covenant, albeit not for nought that is in the world will he fail of the promise he hath made. So they come into the assembly.

X

King Arthur smiteth with his spurs like a good knight and overthroweth two knights in his onset, and Messire Gawain rideth a bandon betwixt two fellowships to be the better known. The most part say, 'See! There is Messire Gawain, the good knight that is King Arthur's nephew.' Nabigant of the Rock cometh toward him as fast as his horse may carry him, lance in rest. Messire Gawain seeth him coming toward him right furiously. He casteth his shield down on the ground and betaketh him to flight as swiftly as he may. They that beheld him, some two score or more, marvel thereof, and say, 'Did ever one see the like overpassing

cowardize!' Nabigant saith that he never and is
yet followed a knight that was vanquished, shamed
nor never will follow one of such conditions,
for no great prize would it be to take him and
win his horse. Other knights come to joust
with him, but Messire Gawain fleeth and
avoideth them the best he may, and maketh
semblance that none is there he durst abide.
He draweth toward King Arthur for safety.
The King hath great shame of this that he
seeth him do, and right sore pains hath he
of defending Messire Gawain, for he holdeth
as close to him as the pie doth to the bramble
when the falcon would take her. In such
shame and dishonour was Messire Gawain as
long as the assembly lasted, and the knights
said that he had gotten him off with much less
than he deserved, for that never had they seen
so craven knight at assembly of tournament as
was he, nor never henceforth would they have
dread of him as they had heretofore. From
this day forward may many lightly avenge
themselves upon him of their kinsfolk and
friends that he hath slain by the forest. The
assembly broke up in the evening, whereof the
King and Messire Gawain were right well
pleased. The knights disarm them at their
hostels and the King and Messire Gawain at
the damsels' tent.

XI

With that, behold you! the dwarf that
cometh. 'By my head, damsels, your knights
go from bad to worse! Of him in the white
arms one may even let pass, but Messire

Gawain is the most coward ever saw I yet, and so he were to run upon me to-morrow and I were armed like as is he, I should think me right well able to defend me against him. 'Tis the devil took him to a place where is such plenty of knights, for the more folk that are there the better may one judge of his ill conditions. And you, Sir,' saith he to the King, 'Wherefore do you keep him company? You would have done best to-day had he not been there. He skulked as close by you, to be out of the buffets, as a hare doth to the wood for the hounds. No business hath good knight to hold company with a coward. I say not this for that I would make him out worse than he is, for I remember the two knights he slew before this tent.' The damsel heareth the dwarf talking and smileth thereat, for she understandeth that blame enough hath Messire Gawain had at the assembly. The knights said at their hostels that they knew not to whom to give the Circlet of Gold, sith that the Knight of the Golden Armour and he of the Red Armour were not there; for they did the best the first day of the assembly, and much they marvelled that they should not come when it was continued on the morrow. 'Gawain,' saith the King, 'Sore blame have you had this day, and I myself have been all shamed for your sake. Never thought I that so good a knight as you might ever have known how to counterfeit a bad knight as you did. You have done much for the love of the damsel, and right well had she avenged herself of you and you had done her great annoy. Howbeit, and **Gawain** to-morrow your cowardize be such as it hath **and** been to-day, never will the day be when you **Arthur** shall not have blame thereof.'

XII

'By my faith,' saith Messire Gawain, 'Behoveth me do the damsel's pleasure sith that we have fallen by ill-chance into her power.' They went to bed at night and took their rest as soon as they had eaten, and on the morrow the damsel came to Messire Gawain. 'I will,' saith she, 'that you be clad in the same arms as was your comrade on the first day, right rich, that I will lend you, and I will, moreover, that you be knight so good as that never on any day were you better. But I command you, by the faith you pledged me the other day, to obey this caution, that you make yourself known to none, and, so any man in the world shall ask your name, you shall say that you are the knight of the Golden Arms.' 'Damsel,' saith Gawain, 'Gramercy! I will do your pleasure.' The younger damsel cometh back to the King: 'Sir,' saith she, 'I will that you wear new arms : You shall bear them red, the same as Messire Gawain bore the first day, and I pray you be such as you were the first day, or better.'

XIII

'Damsel, I will do my best to amend myself and my doings, and right well pleased am I of that it pleaseth you to say.' Their horses were caparisoned and the knights mounted, all armed.

They come together to the tournament with such
an onset as that they pass through the thickest
of the press and overthrew knights and horses
as many as they encountered.   King Arthur
espieth Nabigant that came right gaily caparisoned, and smiteth him so passing strong a
buffet in the midst of his breast that he beareth
him down from his horse, in such sort that
he breaketh his collar-bone, and presenteth the
destrier, by his squire, to the younger damsel,
that maketh great joy thereof.   And Messire
Gawain searcheth the fellowships on all sides,
and so well did he search that scarce was one
might endure his blows.   King Arthur is not
idle, but pierceth shields and beateth in helms,
the while all look on in wonderment at him and
Messire Gawain.   The story saith that the
King would have done still better but that
he put not forth his full strength in deeds of
arms, for that Messire Gawain had done so
ill the day before, and now he would fain that
he should have the prize.

XIV

The damsel that held the Golden Circlet
was in the midst of the assembly of knights, and
had set it in a right rich casket of ivory with
precious stones, right worshipfully.   When the
damsel saw that the assembly was at an end, she
made all the knights stay, and prayed them they
should speak judgment true, concealing nought,
who had best deserved of arms, and ought therefore of right to have the Golden Circlet.   They
said all, that of right judgment the Knight of the

Golden Arms and he of the Red Arms ought to of the
have the prize above all the others, but that of Golden
these two, he of the Golden Arms ought to have Circlet
the prize, for so well did he the first day as
that no knight might do better, and on the last
day likewise, and that if he of the Red Arms had
put forth his full strength on the last day, he
would have done full as well or better. The
Circlet of Gold was brought to Messire Gawain,
but it was not known that it was he; and
Messire Gawain would fain that it had been
given to my lord King Arthur. The knights
departed from the assembly. The King and
Messire Gawain came back to the tent and
brought the Golden Circlet, whereof the damsels
made great joy. Thereupon, behold you! the
dwarf that cometh back. 'Damsels, better is
it to lodge knights such as these than Messire
Gawain the coward, the craven that had so
much shame at the assembly! You yourselves
would have been sore blamed had you lodged
him. This knight hath won the Golden Circlet
by force of arms, and Messire Gawain nought
but shame and reproach.' The damsel laugheth
at this that the dwarf saith, and biddeth him on
his eyes and head, begone!

XV

The King and Messire Gawain were disarmed. 'Sir,' saith the damsel, 'What will you
do with the Golden Circlet?' 'Damsel,' saith
Messire Gawain, 'I will bear it to him that first
won it in sore peril of death, and delivered it to
the Queen that ought to have kept it safe, of

whom it hath been reft by force.' The King and Messire Gawain lay the night in the tent. The younger damsel cometh to the King. 'Sir, many feats of arms have you done at the assembly, as I have been told, for love of me, and I am ready to reward you.' 'Damsel, right great thanks. Your reward and your service love I much, and your honour yet more, wherefore I would that you should have all the honour that any damsel may have, for in damsel without honour ought none to put his affiance. Our Lord God grant you to preserve yours.' 'Damsel,' saith she to the other that sitteth before Messire Gawain, 'This Knight and Messire Gawain have taken counsel together. There is neither solace nor comfort in them. Let us leave them to go to sleep, and ill rest may they have, and Lord God defend us ever hereafter from such guests.' 'By my head,' saith the elder damsel, 'were it not for the Golden Circlet that he is bound of right to deliver again to the Queen that had it in charge, who is my Lady, they should not depart from this land in such sort as they will. But, and Messire Gawain still be nice as concerneth damsels, at least I now know well that he is loyal in another-wise, so as that he will not fail of his word.'

XVI

With that the damsels departed, as did likewise the King and Messire Gawain as soon as they saw the day. Nabigant, that was wounded at the tournament, was borne away on a litter.

Meliot of Logres was in quest of Messire
Gawain. He met the knights and the harness
that came from the assembly, and asked of many
if they could tell him tidings of King Arthur's
nephew, Messire Gawain, and the most part
answer, 'Yea, and right bad tidings enough.'
Then they ask him wherefore he demandeth.
'Lords,' saith he, 'His liege man am I, and
he ought of right to defend my land against all
men, that Nabigant hath taken from me without
right nor reason, whom they are carrying from
thence in a litter, wherefore I am fain to
beseech Messire Gawain that he help me to
recover my land.' 'In faith, Sir Knight,' say
they, 'We know not of what avail he may be
to others that may not help himself. Messire
Gawain was at the assembly, but we tell you
for true, it was he that did worst thereat.'
'Alas,' saith Meliot of Logres, 'Then have I
lost my land, and he hath become even such an
one as you tell me.' 'You would readily
believe us,' say they, 'had you seen him at
the assembly!' Meliot turneth him back, right
sorrowful.

XVII

King Arthur and Messire Gawain depart
from the tent, and come a great pace as though
they fain would escape thence to come nigher
the land where they would be, and great desire
had they of the coming of Lancelot. They
rode until that they came one night to the
Waste Manor whither the brachet led Messire
Gawain when he found the dead knight that

Lancelot had slain. They lodged there the night, and found there knights and damsels of whom they were known. The Lady of the Waste Manor sent for succour to her knights, saying that she held there King Arthur that slew other knights, and that his nephew Messire Gawain was also there within, but dearly would she have loved that Lancelot had been with them that slew her brother. Knights in plenty came to her to do hurt to King Arthur and Messire Gawain, but she had at least so much courtesy in her that she would not suffer any of them to do them ill within her hold, albeit she kept seven of their number, full of great hardiment, to guard the entrance of the bridge, so that King Arthur and Messire Gawain might not depart thence save only amidst the points of their spears.

XVIII

This high history witnesseth us that Lancelot was departed from the Waste City wherein he was much honoured, and rode until that he came to a forest where he met Meliot of Logres, that was sore dismayed of the tidings he had heard of Messire Gawain. Lancelot asketh him whence he cometh, and he saith from seeking Messire Gawain, of whom he had tidings whereof he was right sorrowful. 'How,' saith Lancelot, 'Is he then otherwise than well?' 'Yea,' saith he, 'As I have heard tell : for he wont to be good knight and hath now become evil. He was at the assembly of knights whereof I met the harness

and the fellowships, and they told me that **Lancelot**
never yet was such cowardize in any knight, **and**
but that a knight who was with him did right **Meliot**
well.   But howsoever he may have borne himself, right fain am I to find him, for, maugre
what any may say, I may scarce believe that he
is so bad after all.'   'Sir,' saith Lancelot, 'I
will seek him for you, and you can come along
with me and it seemeth you good.'   Meliot
of Logres betaketh him back with Lancelot.
They ride until they happen by chance upon
the Waste Manor where the King and Messire
Gawain were lodged; and they were armed,
and were minded to go forth from thence.
But the seven knights guarded the issue, all
armed.   The King and Messire Gawain saw
that no good would it do them to remain there
within, wherefore they passed over the bridge
and came perforce to the place where the seven
knights were watching for them.   Thereupon,
they went toward them all armed and struck
among them, and the knights received them on
the points of their lances.

XIX

Thereupon, behold you! Lancelot and the
knight with him, whom they had not been
looking for.   Lancelot espied the King and
Messire Gawain; then the knights cried out
and struck among them as a hawk striketh
amongst larks, and made them scatter on one
side and the other.   Lancelot hath caught one
at his coming, and smiteth him with his spear
through the body, and Meliot of Logres slayeth

another. King Arthur knew Lancelot, and
right glad was he to see him safe and sound, as
was Messire Gawain likewise. Lancelot and
Meliot of Logres made clear the passage for
them. The knights departed, for longer durst
they not abide. The damsel of the castle held
a squire by the hand, that was right passing
comely. She knew Lancelot, and when she
saw him she called him.

XX

'Lancelot, you slew this squire's brother,
and, please God, either he or another shall
take vengeance thereof.' Lancelot holdeth his
peace when he heareth the dame speak, and
departeth from the Waste Hold. Meliot of
Logres knew Messire Gawain and Messire
Gawain him again, and great joy made they
the one of the other. 'Sir,' saith Meliot, 'I
am come to lay plaint before you of Nabigant
of the Rock that challengeth me of the land
whereof I am your man, and saith that he will
defend it against none but you only. Sir, the
day is full nigh, and if you come not to the day,
I shall have lost my quarrel, and you held me
thereof in covenant what time I became your
man.' 'Right fainly will I go,' saith Messire
Gawain. He goeth his way thither accordingly
by leave of the King and Lancelot, and saith
that he will return to them the speediest he
may.

XXI

King Arthur and Lancelot go their way as
fast as they may toward the land that was King

Fisherman's. Messire Gawain rideth until he Gawain
cometh to the land of Nabigant of the Rock. slayeth
Meliot doeth Nabigant to wit that Messire Nabigant
Gawain was come, and that he was ready to
uphold his right by him that was his champion.
Nabigant was whole of the wound he gat at the
assembly, and held Messire Gawain of full
small account for the cowardize that he saw
him do, and bid his knights not meddle betwixt them two, for, and Messire Gawain had
been four knights he thought to vanquish them
all. He issueth forth of his castle all armed,
and is come there where Messire Gawain
awaited him. Messire Gawain seeth him
coming, and so draweth on one side, and
Nabigant, that was stark outrageous, setteth his
spear in rest and cometh toward Messire
Gawain without another word, and smiteth
him on the shield so that he maketh his spear
fly all in pieces. And Messire Gawain catcheth
him right in the midst of his breast, and pierceth
him with his spear through the thick of his
heart, and he falleth to the ground dead; and
the knights run upon Messire Gawain; but he
lightly delivereth himself of them, and Meliot
of Logres likewise. Messire Gawain entereth
the castle by force, doing battle against all the
knights, and holdeth them in such a pass as
that he maketh them do homage to Meliot of
Logres, and deliver up to him the keys of the
castle. He maketh them come to an assembly
from the whole of the land they had reft away
from him, and thereafter departeth and followeth
after King Arthur. In the forest, he over-

taketh a damsel that was going on her way a great pace.

XXII

'Damsel,' saith Messire Gawain, 'Lord God guide you, whither away so fast?' 'Sir,' saith she, 'I am going to the greatest assembly of knights you saw ever.' 'What assembly?' saith Messire Gawain. 'Sir,' saith she, 'At the Palace Meadow, but the knight I am seeking is he that won the Circlet of Gold at the Meadow of the Tent. Fair Sir, can you give me any tidings of him?' saith she. 'Damsel,' saith Messire Gawain, 'What would you do herein?' 'Certes, Sir, I would right fain find him. My Lady, that kept the Circlet of Gold for the son of the Widow Lady, that won it aforetime, hath sent me to seek him.' 'For what intent, damsel?' saith Messire Gawain. 'Sir, my Lady sendeth for him and beseecheth him by me, for the sake of the Saviour of the World, that if he had ever pity of dame or damsel, he will take vengeance on Nabigant that hath slain her men and destroyed her land, for she hath been told how he that won back the Golden Circlet ought of right to take vengeance upon him.'

XXIII

'Damsel,' saith Messire Gawain, 'Be not any longer troubled hereof, for I tell you that the knight that won the Golden Circlet by prize of arms hath killed Nabigant already.' 'Sir,' saith she, 'How know you this?' 'I know the knight well,' saith he, 'And I saw

him slay him, and behold, here is the Circlet Evil tidings
of Gold that I have as a token hereof, for that
he beareth it to him that hath won the Graal,
to the intent that your Lady may be quit of her
charge.' Messire Gawain showeth her the
Golden Circlet in the casket of ivory, that he
kept very nigh himself. Right joyful was the
damsel that the matter had thus fallen out, and
goeth her way back again to tell her Lady of
her joy. Messire Gawain goeth on his way
toward the assembly, for well knoweth he that,
and King Arthur and Lancelot have heard the
tidings, there will they be. He goeth thitherward as fast as he may, and as straight, and
scarce hath he ridden away or ever he met a
squire that seemed right weary, and his hackney
sore worn of the way. Messire Gawain asked
him whence he came, and the squire said to
him, 'From the land of King Arthur, where
is great war toward, for that none knoweth not
what hath become of him. Many folk go about
saying that he is dead, for never sithence that
he departed from Cardoil, and Messire Gawain
and Lancelot with him, have no tidings been
heard of him ; and he left the Queen at Cardoil
to take his place, and also on account of her
son's death, and the most part say that he is
dead. Briant of the Isles and my Lord Kay
with him are burning his land, and carrying
off plunder before all the castles. Of all the
Knights of the Table Round are there now no
more than five and thirty, and of these are ten
sore wounded, and they are in Cardoil, and there
protect the land the best they may.'

XXIV

When Messire Gawain heareth these tidings,
they touch his heart right sore, so that he goeth
the straightest he may toward the assembly,
and the squire with him that was sore for-
done.   Messire Gawain found King Arthur and
Lancelot, and the knights were come from all
the kingdom to the piece of ground.   For a
knight was come thither that had brought a
white destrier and borne thither a right rich
crown of gold, and it was known throughout all
the lands that marched with this, that the knight
that should do best at the assembly should have
the destrier and the crown, for the Queen that
ware it was dead, and it would behove him to
guard and defend the land whereof she had been
Lady.   On account of these tidings had come
thither great plenty of folk and of folk.   King
Arthur and Messire Gawain and Lancelot set
them of one side.   The story saith that at this
assembly King Arthur bare the red shield that
the damsel gave him; Messire Gawain had his
own, such as he was wont to bear, and Lancelot
a green shield that he bare for the love of the
knight that was slain for helping him in the
forest.   They struck into the assembly like
lions unchained, and cast down three knights
at their first onset.   They searched the fellowships on every side, smote down knights and
overthrew horses.

XXV

King Arthur overtook no knight but he clave
his shield to the boss; all swerved aside and

avoided his buffets. And Messire Gawain and **a dolorous** Lancelot are not idle on the other hand, but **prize** each held well his place. But the more part had wonderment looking at the King, for he holdeth him at bay like a lion when the staghounds would attack him. The assembly lasted throughout on such wise, and when it came to an end, the knights said and adjudged that the Knight of the Red Shield had surpassed all other in doing well. The knight that had brought the crown came to the King, but knew him not a whit : 'Sir,' saith he, 'You have by your good deeds of arms won this crown of gold and this destrier, whereof ought you to make great joy, so only you have so much valour in you as that you may defend the land of the best earthly Queen that is dead, and whether the King be alive or dead none knoweth, wherefore great worship will it be to yourself and you may have prowess to maintain the land, for right broad is it and right rich and of high sovranty.'

XXVI

Saith King Arthur, 'Whose was the land, and what was the name of the Queen whose crown I see?' 'Sir, the King's name was Arthur, and the best king in the world was he; but in his kingdom the more part say that he is dead. And this crown was the crown of Queen Guenievre that is dead and buried, whereof is sore sorrow. The knights that may not leave Cardoil lest Briant of the Isles should seize the city, they sent me to the kingdom of Logres and charged me with the crown and destrier for

A
grievous
sorrow
that I have knowledge of the isles and foreign lands; wherefore they prayed me I should go among the assemblies of knights, that so I might hear tidings of my Lord King Arthur and my Lord Gawain and Lancelot, and, so I might find them, that I should tell them how the land hath fallen into this grievous sorrow.' King Arthur heareth tidings whereof he is full sorrowful. He draweth on one side, and the knights make the most grievous dole in the world. Lancelot knoweth not what he may do, and saith between his teeth that now hath his joy come to an end and his knighthood is of no avail, for that he hath lost the high Queen, the valiant, that heart and comfort gave him and encouragement to do well. The tears ran down from his comely eyes right amidst his face and through the ventail, and, had he durst make other dole, yet greater would it have been. Of the mourning the King made is there nought to speak, for this sorrow resembleth none other. He holdeth the crown of gold, and looketh full oft at the destrier for love of her, for he had given it her; and Messire Gawain may not stint of making dole.

XXVII

'Certes,' saith he, 'Now may I well say that the best Queen in the world and of most understanding is dead, nor never hereafter shall be none of equal worth.' 'Sir,' saith Lancelot to the King, 'So it please you, and Messire Gawain be willing, I will go back toward Cardoil, and help to defend your land to the best I may, for

sore is it discounselled, until such time as you **Lancelot**
shall be come from the Graal.' 'Certes,' saith **returneth**
Messire Gawain to the King, 'Lancelot hath
spoken well, so you grant him your consent.'
'That do I with right good will,' saith the
King, 'And I pray him right heartily that he
go thither and be guardian of my land and the
governance thereof, until such time as God shall
have brought me back.' Lancelot taketh leave
of the King and goeth his way back, all sorrowing and full of discontent.

BRANCH XXII

Perce-val's castle OF Lancelot the story is here silent, and so beginneth another branch of the Graal in the name of the Father, and of the Son, and of the Holy Ghost.

TITLE I

You may well understand that King Arthur is no whit joyful. He maketh the white destrier go after him, and hath the crown of gold full near himself. They ride until they come to the castle that belonged to King Fisherman, and they found it as rich and fair as you have heard told many a time. Perceval, that was there within, made right great joy of their coming, as did all the priests and ancient knights. Perceval leadeth King Arthur, when he was disarmed, into the chapel where the Graal was, and Messire Gawain maketh present to Perceval of the Golden Circlet, and telleth him that the Queen sendeth it to him, and relateth also how Nabigant had seized it, and moreover, how Nabigant was dead. The King offereth the crown that had been Queen Guenievre's. When Perceval knew that she was dead, he was right sorrowful thereof in his heart, and wept and lamented her right sweetly. He showeth them the tomb of King Fisherman,

110

and telleth them that none had set the tabernacle
there above the coffin, but only the commandment of Our Lord, and he showeth them a rich
pall that is upon the coffin, and telleth them that
every day they see a new one there not less rich
than is this one. King Arthur looketh at the
sepulchre and saith that never tofore hath he
seen none so costly. A smell issueth therefrom
full delicate and sweet of savour. The King
sojourneth in the castle and is highly honoured,
and beholdeth the richesse and the lordship and
the great abundance that is everywhere in the
castle, insomuch that therein is nought wanting
that is needful for the bodies of noble folk.
Perceval had made set the bodies of the dead
knights in a charnel beside an old chapel in the
forest, and the body of his uncle that had slain
himself so evilly. Behind the castle was a
river, as the history testifieth, whereby all good
things came to the castle, and this river was
right fair and plenteous. Josephus witnesseth
us that it came from the Earthly Paradise and
compassed the castle around and ran on through
the forest as far as the house of a worshipful
hermit, and there lost the course and had peace
in the earth. All along the valley thereof was
great plenty of everything continually, and
nought was ever lacking in the rich castle
that Perceval had won. The castle, so saith
the history, had three names.

II

One of the names was Eden, the second,
Castle of Joy, and the third, Castle of Souls.

The bell and chalice Now Josephus saith that none never passed away therein but his soul went to Paradise. King Arthur was one day at the castle windows with Messire Gawain. The King seeth coming before him beyond the bridge a great procession of folk one before another; and he that came before was all clad in white, and bare a full great cross, and each of the others a little one, and the more part came singing with sweet voices and bear candles burning, and there was one behind that carried a bell with the clapper and all at his neck. 'Ha, God,' saith King Arthur, 'What folk be these?' 'Sir,' saith Perceval, 'I know them all save the last. They are the hermits of this forest, that come to chant within yonder before the Holy Graal, three days in the week.'

III

When the hermits came nigh the castle, the King went to meet them, and the knights adore the crosses and bow their heads before the good men. As soon as they were come into the holy chapel, they took the bell from the last and smote thereon at the altar, and then set it on the ground, and then began they the service, most holy and most glorious. The history witnesseth us that in the land of King Arthur at this time was there not a single chalice. The Graal appeared at the sacring of the mass, in five several manners that none ought not to tell, for the secret things of the sacrament ought none to tell openly but he to whom God hath given it. King Arthur beheld

all the changes, the last whereof was the change
into a chalice. And the hermit that chanted
the mass found a brief under the corporal
and declared the letters, to wit, that our Lord
God would that in such vessel should His body
be sacrificed, and that it should be set upon
record. The history saith not that there were
no chalices elsewhere, but that in all Great
Britain and in the whole kingdom was none.
King Arthur was right glad of this that he had
seen, and had in remembrance the name and the
fashion of the most holy chalice. Then he
asked the hermit that bare the bell, whence
this thing came? 'Sir,' saith he to Messire
Gawain, 'I am the King for whom you slew
the giant, whereby you had the sword wherewith St. John was beheaded, that I see on this
altar. I made baptize me before you and all
those of my kingdom, and turn to the New
Law, and thereafter I went to a hermitage by
the sea, far from folk, where I have been of a
long space. I rose one night at matins and
looked under my hermitage and saw that a ship
had taken haven there. I went thither when
the sea was retreated, and found within the ship
three priests and their clerks, that told me their
names and how they were called in baptism.
All three were named Gregory, and they came
from the Land of Promise, and told me that
Solomon had cast three bells, one for the Saviour
of the World, and one for His sweet Mother, and
one for the honour of His saints, wherefore
they had brought this hither by His commandment into this kingdom for that we had none

here. They told me that and I should bear it
into this castle, they would take all my sins
upon themselves, by Our Lord's pleasure, in
such sort as that I should be quit thereof. And
I in like manner have brought it hither by the
commandment of God, who willeth that this
should be the pattern of all those that shall be
fashioned in the realm of this island where never
aforetime have been none.' 'By my faith,'
saith Messire Gawain to the hermit, 'I know
you right well for a worshipful man, for you
held your covenant truly with me.' King
Arthur was right glad of this thing, as were
all they that were within. It seemed him
that the noise thereof was like the noise that he
had heard sound ever since he had moved from
Cardoil. The hermits went their way each to
his hermitage when they had done the service.

IV

One day, as the King sate at meat in the hall
with Perceval and Messire Gawain and the
ancient knights, behold you therewithal one of
the three Damsels of the Car that cometh, and
she was smitten all through her right arm.
'Sir,' saith she to Perceval, 'Have mercy on
your mother and your sister and on us. Aristot
of Moraine, that is cousin to the Lord of the
Moors that you slew, warreth upon your mother,
and hath carried off your sister by force into the
castle of a vavasour of his, and saith that he will
take her to wife, and will have all her land that
your mother ought to hold of right, maugre
your head. But never had knight custom so

cruel as he, for when he shall have espoused **The two**
the damsel, whomsoever she may be, yet will **Camelots**
he never love her so well but that he shall cut off
her head with his own hand, and so thereafter
go seek for another to slay in like manner.
Natheless in one matter hath he good custom,
that never will he do shame to none until such
time as he hath espoused her. Sir, I was with
my Lady your sister when he maimed me in
this manner. Wherefore your mother sendeth
you word and prayeth you that you succour her,
for you held her in covenant that so you would
do and she should have need thereof and you
should know it; for and you consent to her
injury and loss, the shame will be your own.'
Perceval heard these tidings, and sore sorrowful
was he thereof. 'By my head,' saith the King
to Perceval, 'I and my nephew, so please you,
will go to help you.' 'Sir,' saith he, 'Gramercy, but go and achieve your own affair also,
for sore need have you thereof; wherefore I
pray and beseech you that you be guardian of
the castle of Camelot, if that my lady mother
shall come thither, for thereof make I you lord
and champion, and albeit the castle be far away
from you, yet garnish it and guard it, for it is
builded in a place right fair.'

v

Lords, think not that it is this Camelot
whereof these tellers of tales do tell their tales,
there, where King Arthur so often held his
court. This Camelot that was the Widow
Lady's stood upon the uttermost headland of

Arthur's
Camelot

the wildest isle of Wales by the sea to the West. Nought was there save the hold and the forest and the waters that were round about it.   The other Camelot, of King Arthur's, was situate at the entrance of the kingdom of Logres, and was peopled of folk and was seated at the head of the King's land, for that he had in his governance all the lands that on that side marched with his own.

TITLE I

OF Perceval the story is here silent, and Arthur saith that King Arthur and Messire and Gawain have taken leave of Perceval and all them of the castle. The King leaveth him the good destrier that he won, with the golden crown. They have ridden, he and Messire Gawain together, until they are come to a waste ancient castle that stood in a forest. The castle would have been right fair and rich had any folk wonned therein, but none there were save one old priest and his clerk that lived within by their own toil. The King and Messire Gawain lodged there the night, and on the morrow went into a right rich chapel . that was therein to hear mass, and it was painted all around of right rich colours of gold and azure and other colours. The images were right fair that were there painted, and the figures of them for whom the images were made. The King and Messire Gawain looked at them gladly. When the mass was said, the priest cometh to them and saith : 'Lords,' saith he, 'These imagings are right fair, and he that had them made is full loyal, and dearly loved the lady and her son for whom he had them made. Sir,' saith the priest, 'It is a true history.' 'Of whom is the history, fair Sir?'

A strange story saith King Arthur. 'Of a worshipful vavasour that owned this hold, and of Messire Gawain, King Arthur's nephew, and his mother. Sir,' saith the priest, 'Messire Gawain was born there within and held up and baptized, as you may see here imaged, and he was named Gawain for the sake of the lord of this castle that had that name. His mother, that had him by King Lot, would not that it should be known. She set him in a right fair coffer, and prayed the good man of this castle that he would carry him away and leave him where he might perish, but and if he would not do so, she would make another do it. This Gawain, that was loyal and would not that the child should be put to death, made seal letters at the pillow-bere of his cradle that he was of lineage royal on the one side and the other, and set therein gold and silver so as that the child might be nurtured in great plenty, and spread above the child a right rich coverlid. He carried him away to a far distant country, and so came one early morning to a little homestead where dwelt a right worshipful man. He delivered the child to him and his wife, and bade them they should keep him and nurture him well, and told them that it might be much good should come to them thereof. The vavasour turned him back, and they took charge of the child and nurtured him until that he were grown, and then took him to Rome to the Holy Father and showed him the sealed letters. The Holy Father saw them and understood that he was the son of a King. He had pity upon him, and gave him to understand that he was of his kindred. After that, he was elected to be Emperor of Rome. But he would not be Emperor lest he should be reproached of his birth that had before been concealed from him. He departed thence, and lived afterwards within yonder. Now is it said that he is one of the best knights in the world, insomuch that none durst take possession of this castle for dread of him, nor of this great forest that lieth round about it. For, when the vavasour that dwelt here was dead, he left to Messire Gawain, his foster-son, this castle, and made me guardian thereof until such time as Messire Gawain should return.'

II

The King looketh at Messire Gawain, and seeth him stoop his head toward the ground for shame. 'Fair nephew, be not ashamed, for as well might you reproach me of the same. Of your birth hath there been great joy, and dearly ought one to love the place and honour it, where so good a knight as are you was born.' When the priest understood that it was Messire Gawain, he made great cheer to him, and was all shamed of that he had recorded as concerning his birth. But he saith to him: 'Sir, small blame ought you to have herein, for you were confirmed in the law that God hath established and in loyalty of marriage of King Lot and your mother. This thing King Arthur well knoweth, and our Lord God be praised for that you have come hither!'

Of Meliant HERE the story is silent of the kingdom, and of King Arthur and Messire Gawain that remain in the castle to maintain and guard it until they shall have garnished it of folk. Here speaketh it word of the knight's son of the Waste Manor, there whither the brachet led Messire Gawain where he found the knight that Lancelot had slain. He had one son whose name was Meliant, and he had not forgotten his father's death; rather, thereof did wrath rankle in his heart. He heard tell that Briant of the Isles had great force and great puissance, and that he warred upon King Arthur's land, insomuch as that he had already slain many of his knights. Thitherward goeth he, and is come to where Briant was in a castle of his own. He telleth him how Lancelot had slain his father in such sort, and prayeth him right courteously that he would make him knight, for that right fain would he avenge his father, and therefore would he help him in the war the best he might. Briant made much joy thereof, and made him knight in right costly sort, and he was the comeliest knight and the most valiant of his age in Briant's court, and greatly did he desire to meet with Lancelot. They marvelled much in the land and kingdom

120

what had become of him. The more part and
thought that he was dead, albeit dead he was Lancelot
not, but rather sound and hale and whole, had
it not been for the death of Queen Guenievre,
whereof the sorrow so lay at his heart that he
might not forget it. He rode one day amidst
a forest, and overtook a knight and a damsel
that made great joy together, singing and making
disport. 'By God,' saith the damsel, 'If this
knight that cometh here will remain, he shall
have right good lodging. It is already nigh
eventide, and never will he find hostel so good
to-day.' 'Damsel,' saith Lancelot, 'Of good
hostel have I sore need, for I am more than
enough weary.' 'So be all they,' saith she,
'that come from the land of the rich King
Fisherman, for none may suffer the pain and
travail and he be not good knight.'

II

'Ah, damsel,' saith Lancelot, 'Which is the
way to the castle whereof you speak?' 'Sir,'
saith the knight, 'You will go by this cross
that you see before you, and we will go by that
other way, to a certain hold. Haply we shall
find you at the castle or ever you depart thence.'
Lancelot goeth his way and leaveth them. 'By
my head,' saith the damsel to the knight, 'This
that goeth there is Lancelot. He knoweth me
not, albeit I know him well, and I hear that he
is sore troubled of his sorrow and mis-ease.
Natheless, please God, I will have vengeance
of him or ever he departeth from the castle
whither he goeth to harbour. He made marry

The Castle of Griffons perforce a knight that loved me better than aught beside, and to a damsel that he loved not a whit. And so much might he still better perceive when he saw that she ate not at his table, but was seated along with the squires, and that none did aught for her at the castle. But the knight will not abandon her for his own honour, and for that I should be blamed thereof.' The evening draweth on and Lancelot goeth toward the castle, that was right uneath to find and in an unfrequented part. He espieth it at the head of the forest, and seeth that it is large and strong, with strong barbicans embattelled, and at the entrance of the gateway were fifteen heads of knights hanging. He found without a knight that came from the forest, and asked him what castle it was, and he made answer that it was called the Castle of the Griffon. 'And why are these heads hanging at this door?' 'Sir,' saith he, 'The daughter of the lord of the castle is the fairest in the world and that is known in any kingdom, and needs must she be offered to wife to all knights that harbour within. He that can draw a sword that is fixed in a column in the midst of the hall, and fetch it forth, he shall have her of right without forfeit.

III

'All these have made assay whose heads you see hanging at the door, but never might none of them remove the sword, and on this occasion were they beheaded. Now is it said that none may draw it forth, unless he that draweth be

better knight than another, and needs must he **Lancelot**
be one of them that have been at the Graal. **lodgeth**
But, and you be minded to believe me, fair Sir,' **therein**
saith the knight, 'You will go elsewhither, for
ill lodging is it in a place where one must needs
set body and life in adventure of death, and
none ought to be blamed for escaping from his
own harm. Sir, the castle is right fell, for it
hath underground, at the issue of a cavern that
is there, a lion and a griffon that have devoured
more than half a hundred knights.' 'Sir,'
saith Lancelot, 'It is evening, nor know I how
I may go farther this day, for I know not
whither to go sith that I know not the places
nor the ways of the forest.' 'Sir,' saith the
knight, 'I speak only for your own good, and
God grant you depart hence, honour safe.'
Lancelot findeth the door of the castle all open,
and entereth in, all armed, and alighteth before
the master-hall. The King was leaning at the
windows, and biddeth stall his horse.

IV

Lancelot is entered into the hall, and findeth
knights and damsels at the tables and playing at
the chess, but none did he find to salute him nor
make him cheer of his coming save the lord
only, for such was the custom of the castle.
The lord bade him be disarmed. 'Sir,' saith
he, 'Right well may you allow me wear my
arms, for they be the fairest garniture and the
richest I have.' 'Sir,' saith the lord of the
castle, 'No knight eateth armed within yonder,
but he that cometh armed in hither disarmeth

himself by my leave.   He may take his arms
again without gainsay so neither I nor other
desire to do him a hurt.'   With that two squires
disarm him.   The lord of the castle maketh
bring a right rich robe wherein to apparel him.
The tables were set and the meats served.   The
damsel issued forth of her chamber and was
accompanied of two knights as far as the hall.
She looketh at Lancelot, and seeth that he is a
right comely knight, and much liketh her of
his bearing and countenance, and she thinketh
to herself that sore pity would it be so comely
knight should have his head smitten off.

V

Lancelot saluted the damsel and made great
cheer, and when they had eaten in hall, forthwith behold you, the damsel where she cometh
that Lancelot overtook in the forest with the
knight. 'Sir,' saith she to the lord of the
castle, 'You have harboured this night your
deadly enemy that slew your brother at the
Waste Manor.' 'By my faith,' saith the lord
of the manor, 'I think not so, for him would
I not have harboured, nor will I not believe
it for true until such time as I have proved it.
Sir,' saith he to Lancelot, 'Make the demand
that the others make!' 'What is it?' saith
Lancelot. 'See there my daughter! Ask her
of me, and if you be such as you ought to be,
I will give her to you.' 'Sir,' saith Lancelot,
'No knight is there in the world so good but
ought to plume him upon having her to wife,
so always she were willing, and, so I thought

that you would be willing to give her to me,
I would willingly ask you.' Lancelot spake
otherwise than as he thought, for the departing
of the Queen and the sorrow thereof lay so
at his heart that never again might he lean upon
any love in the world, neither of dame nor
damsel. He asked his daughter of the knight
of the castle, and came before him to save
the custom so that he might not have blame
thereof. And he showed him the sword that
is in the column, all inlaid with gold. 'Go,'
saith he, 'and fulfil the custom, as other knights
have done.' 'What is it?' saith Lancelot.
'They might not draw forth the sword from
this column, and so failed of my daughter and
of their lives.' 'Lord God,' saith Lancelot,
'Defend me from this custom!' And he
cometh toward the column as fast as he may,
and seizeth the sword with both hands. So
soon as he touched it, the sword draweth it
forth with such a wrench that the column
quaked thereof. The damsel was right joyful
thereat, albeit she misdoubted the fellness and
cruelty of her father, for never yet had she
seen knight that pleased her so much to love
as he. 'Sir,' saith the other damsel, 'I tell
you plainly, this is Lancelot, the outrageous,
that slew your brother. Natheless, is it no
lie that he is one of the best knights of the
world, albeit by the stoutness of his knighthood
and his valour many an outrage hath he done,
and more shall he yet do and he escape you,
and, so you will believe me, you will never
allow him to depart thus; sith that and you

*Lancelot
draweth
a sword*

A kill him or slay him you will save the life of
damsel many a knight.' The daughter of the lord of
loveth the castle is sore displeased of the damsel for
Lancelot this that she saith, and looketh at Lancelot
from time to time and sigheth, but more durst
she not do. Much marvelleth she, sith that
Lancelot hath drawn the sword forth of the
column, that he asketh her not of her father as
his own liege woman, but he was thinking of
another thing, and never was he so sorrowful of
any lady as he was for the Queen. But whatsoever thought or desire he may have therein,
he telleth the lord of the castle that he holdeth
him to his covenant made at such time as the
sword was still fixed in the column. 'I have
a right not to hold thereto,' saith the lord of the
castle, 'Nor shall I break not my vow and I
fail you herein; for no man is bound to give
his daughter to his mortal enemy. Sith that
you have slain my brother, you are my mortal
enemy, and were I to give her to you, she
ought not to wish it, and were she to grant you
her love she would be a fool and a madwoman.'
Right sorrowful is the damsel of this that she
heareth her father say. She would fain that
Lancelot and she were in the forest, right in
the depth thereof. But Lancelot had no mind
to be as she was thinking. The lord of the
castle made guard the gateway of the castle
well, in such sort that Lancelot might issue
therefrom on no side. Afterward he bade his
knights privily that they take heed on their
lives that they be all ready on the morrow and
all garnished of their arms, for that it was his

purpose to smite off Lancelot's head and hang **and**
it above all the others.   **sendeth**
him
counsel

VI

The daughter of the lord knew these tidings
and was right sorrowful thereof, for she thinketh
never more to have joy at heart and he shall
be slain in such manner. She sendeth him
greeting by her own privy messenger, as she
that loveth him better than aught else living in
the world, and so biddeth and prayeth him be
garnished of his arms, and ready to protect his
life, for that her father is fain to smite off his
head. 'Sir,' saith the messenger, 'Your force
would avail you nought as against my lord, for
to-morrow there will be a dozen knights all
armed at the issue of the gate whereby you
entered to-night, and he saith that he purposeth
to cut off your head there where he cut the
heads off the other knights. Without the gate
there will likewise be another dozen knights all
armed. No knight is there in the world so
good as that he might issue forth of this castle
through the midst of these four and twenty
knights, but my lady sendeth you word that
there is a cavern under this castle that goeth
therefrom underground as far as the forest, so
that a knight may well pass thereby all armed,
but there is therein a lion, the fiercest and most
horrible in the world, and two serpents that are
called griffons, that have the face of a man and
the beaks of birds and eyes of an owl and teeth
of a dog and ears of an ass and feet of a lion
and tail of a serpent, and they have couched

Lancelot
misliketh
it them therewithin, but never saw no man beasts
so fell and felonous.   Wherefore the damsel
biddeth you go by that way, by everything that
you have ever loved, and that you fail her not,
for she would fain speak with you at the issue
of the cavern in an orchard that is nigh a right
broad river not far from this castle, and will
make your destrier be brought after you underground.' 'By my head,' saith Lancelot, 'And
she had not conjured me in such sort, and were
it not for love of herself, I would have rather set
myself in hazard with the knights than with
the wild beasts, for far fainer would I have
delivered myself from them, and so I might,
than go forth in such-wise.'   'She sendeth you
word,' saith the messenger, 'that so you do not
thus, no further trouble will she take concerning
you.   She doth it of dread lest she lose your
love; and here behold a brachet that she
sendeth you by me that you will carry with
you into the cavern.   So soon as you shall
see the serpent griffons that have couched them
therein, you shall show them this and cast her
down before them.   The griffons love her as
much as one beast may love another, and shall
have such joy and such desire to play with the
brachet that they will leave you alone, and have
such good will toward you that they will not
look at you after to do you any hurt.   But no
man is there in the world, no matter how well
soever he were armed, nor how puissant soever
he were in himself, might never pass them
otherwise, but he should be devoured of them.
But no safeguard may you have as against the

lion but of God only and your own hardiment.' *but escapeth thereby* 'Tell my damsel,' saith Lancelot, 'that all her commandment will I do, but this cowardize resembleth none other, that I shall go fight with beasts and leave to do battle with knights.' This was then repeated to the damsel, that marvelled her much thereat, and said that he was the hardiest knight in the world.

VII

Lancelot armed him toward daybreak, and had his sword girt, his shield at his neck, and his spear in his hand. So he entered into the cavern, all shamefast, and the brachet followeth after, that he deigned not to carry, and so cometh he to the place where the griffons were. So soon as they heard him coming they dress them on their feet, and then writhe along as serpents, then cast forth such fire, and so bright a flame amidst the rock, as that all the cavern is lighted up thereof, and they see by the brightness of light of their jaws the brachet coming. So soon as they have espied her, they carry her in their claws and make her the greatest cheer in the world. Lancelot passeth beyond without gainsay, and espieth, toward the issue of the cavern, the lion that was come from the forest all famished. He cometh thither right hardily, sword drawn. The lion cometh toward him, jaws yawning, and claws bared, thinking to fix them in his habergeon, but Lancelot preventeth him and smiteth him so stoutly that he cutteth off thigh and leg together. When the lion feeleth himself thus

maimed, he seizeth him by the teeth and the
claws of his fore feet and rendeth away half
the skirt of his habergeon. Thereupon Lancelot waxeth wroth. He casteth his shield to
the ground and approacheth the lion closer.
He seeth that he openeth his jaws wide to
avenge himself, and thrusteth his sword the
straightest he may into his gullet, and the lion
giveth out a roar and falleth dead. The damsel,
that had come into the cavern, heareth that the
lion is dead.

VIII

Lancelot issueth forth and so cometh into
the orchard beside the forest, and wiped his
sword on the freshness of the green grass.
Thereupon behold you the damsel that cometh.
'Sir,' saith she to Lancelot, 'Are you wounded
in any place?' 'Damsel, nowhere, thank
God!' Another damsel leadeth a horse
into the orchard. The damsel of the castle
looketh at Lancelot. 'Sir,' saith the damsel,
'Meseemeth that you are not over joyous.'
'Damsel,' saith he, 'If I be not, I have good
right, for I have lost the thing in the world that
most I loved.' 'And you have won me,' saith
she, 'so you remain not here, that am the
fairest damsel in this kingdom, and I have
saved you your life for this, that you grant me
your love, for mine own would I fain give to
you.' 'Gramercy, damsel,' saith Lancelot,
'Your love and your good will fain would I
have; but neither you nor none other damsel
ought not to have affiance in me, and I might

so soon set carelessly aside the love to whom and
my heart owed its obedience, for the worthiness
and the courtesy that were lodged in her.   Nor
never hereafter, so long as I live, shall I love
none other in like manner ; wherefore all others
commend I to God, and to yourself, as for
leave-taking to one at whose service I fain
would be ; I say that if you shall have need
of me, and so I be in place and free, I will
do all I may to protect your honour.'

*and
denieth
the
damsel*

IX

'Ha, God!' saith the damsel, 'How am I
betrayed, sith that I am parted from the best
knight in the world!   Lancelot, you have done
that which never yet no knight might do!
Now am I grieved that you should escape on
such wise, and that your life hath been saved in
this manner by me.   Better should I love you
mine own dead, than another's living.   Now
would I fain that you had had your head
smitten off, and that it were hanging with the
others!   So would I solace myself by beholding
it!'   Lancelot took no account of that he heard,
for the grief that lay at his heart of the Queen.
He mounteth on his horse and issueth forth of
the orchard by a postern gate, and entereth into
the forest, and commendeth him to God.   The
lord of the Castle of the Griffons marvelleth
much that Lancelot delayeth so long.   He
thinketh that he durst not come down, and
saith to his knights, 'Let us go up and cut off
his head, sith that he durst not come down.'
He maketh search for him all through the hall

and the chambers, but findeth him not. 'He
hath gone,' saith he, 'through the cavern, so
have the griffons devoured him.' So he sendeth
the twain most hardy of his knights to see.
But the brachet had returned after the damsel,
whereof the griffons were wroth, and they
forthwith seized on the two knights that entered
into their cavern and slew them and devoured.

X

When the lord of the castle knew it, he
went into the chamber where his daughter was,
and found her weeping, and thinketh that it is
for the two knights that are dead. News is
brought him that the lion is dead at the issue of
the cavern, and thereby well knoweth he that
Lancelot is gone. He biddeth his knights
follow after him, but none was there so hardy
as that he durst follow. The damsel was right
fain they should go after him, if only they
might bring him back to the castle, for so
mortally was she taken of his love that she
thought of none other thing. But Lancelot
had her not in remembrance, but only another,
and rode on sadly right amidst the forest, and
looked from time to time at the rent the lion
had made in his habergeon. He rideth until he
is come toward evening to a great valley where
was forest on the one side and the other, and
the valley stretched onward half a score great
leagues Welsh. He looketh to the right, and
on the top of the mountain beside the valley he
seeth a chapel newly builded that was right fair

and rich, and it was covered of lead, and had
at the back two quoins that seemed to be of
gold. By the side of this chapel were three
houses dight right richly, each standing by
itself facing the chapel. There was a right
fair grave-yard round about the chapel, that
was enclosed at the compass of the forest, and
a spring came down, full clear, from the
heights of the forest before the chapel and
ran into the valley with a great rushing; and
each of the houses had its own orchard, and
the orchard an enclosure. Lancelot heareth
vespers being chanted in the chapel, and seeth
the path that turned thitherward, but the
mountain is so rugged that he could not go
along it on horseback. So he alighteth, and
leadeth his horse after him by the reins until
he cometh nigh the chapel.

XI

There were three hermits therewithin that
had sung their vespers, and came over against
Lancelot. They bowed their heads to him
and he saluted them, and then asked of them
what place was this? And they told him that
the place there was Avalon. They make stable
his horse. He left his arms without the chapel
and entereth therein, and saith that never hath
he seen none so fair nor so rich. There were
within three other places, right fair and seemly
dight of rich cloths of silk and rich corners and
fringes of gold. He seeth the images and the
crucifixes all newly fashioned, and the chapel

The two illumined of rich colours; and moreover in the
coffins midst thereof were two coffins, one against the
other, and at the four corners four tall wax
tapers burning, that were right rich, in four right
rich candlesticks. The coffins were covered
with two palls, and there were clerks that
chanted psalms in turn on the one side and
the other. 'Sir,' saith Lancelot to one of the
hermits, 'For whom were these coffins made?'
'For King Arthur and Queen Guinievre.'
'King Arthur is not yet dead,' saith Lancelot.
'No, in truth, please God! but the body of
the Queen lieth in the coffin before us, and in
the other is the head of her son, until such
time as the King shall be ended, to whom God
grant long life! But the Queen bade at her
death that his body should be set beside her
own when he shall end. Hereof have we the
letters and her seal in this chapel, and this
place made she be builded new on this wise or
ever she died.'

XII

When Lancelot heareth that it is the Queen
that lieth in the coffin, he is so straitened in his
heart and in his speech that never a word may
he say. But no semblant of grief durst he
make other than such as might not be perceived,
and right great comfort to him was it that there
was an image of Our Lady at the head of the
coffin. He knelt down the nighest he might
to the coffin, as it had been to worship the
image, and set his face and his mouth to the
stone of the coffin, and sorroweth for her right

sweetly. 'Ha, Lady,' saith he, 'But that I **Lancelot**
dread the blame of the people, never again **his vigil**
would I seek to depart from this place, but
here would I save my soul and pray for yours;
so would it be much recomforting to me that I
should be so nigh, and should see the sepulchre
wherein your body lieth that had so great
sweetness and bounty. God, grant me of your
pleasure, that at my death I may still be a-nigh,
and that I may die in such manner and in such
place as that I may be shrouded and buried in
this holy chapel where this body lieth.' The
night cometh on. A clerk cometh to the
hermits and saith, 'Never yet did no knight
cry mercy of God so sweetly, nor of His sweet
Mother, as did this knight that is in the chapel.'
And the hermits make answer that knights for
the most part do well believe in God. They
come to the chapel for him and bid him come
thence, for that meat is ready and he should
come to eat, and after that go to sleep and rest,
for it is full time so to do. He telleth them
that as for his eating this day it is stark nought,
for a desire and a will hath taken him to keep
vigil in the chapel before one of the images of
Our Lady. No wish had he once to depart
thence before the day, and he would fain that
the night should last far longer than it did.
The good men durst not force him against his
will; they say, rather, that the worshipful man is
of good life who will keep watch in such manner
throughout the night without drink or meat, for
all that he seemeth to be right weary.

XIII

Lancelot was in the chapel until the morrow
before the tomb. The hermits apparelled them
to do the service that they chanted each day,
mass for the soul of the Queen and her son.
Lancelot heareth them with right good will.
When the masses were sung, he taketh leave of
the hermits and looketh at the coffin right
tenderly. He commendeth the body that lieth
therein to God and His sweet Mother; then
findeth he without the chapel his horse accoutred
ready, and mounteth forthwith, and departeth,
and looketh at the place and the chapel so long
as he may see them. He hath ridden so far
that he is come nigh Cardoil, and findeth the
land wasted and desolate, and the towns burnt,
whereof is he sore grieved. He meeteth a
knight that came from that part, and he was
wounded full sore. Lancelot asketh him
whence he cometh, and he saith, 'Sir, from
towards Cardoil. Kay the Seneschal, with
two other knights, is leading away Messire
Ywain li Aoutres toward the castle of the Hard
Rock. I thought to help to rescue him, but
they have wounded me in such sort as you see.'
'Are they ever so far away?' saith Lancelot.
' Sir, they will pass just now at the head of this
forest; and so you are fain to go thither, I will
return with you right willingly and help you to
the best I may.' Lancelot smiteth his horse with
the spurs forthwith, and the knight after him,
and espieth Kay the Seneschal, that was bringing Messire Ywain along at a great pace, and

had set him upon a trotting hackney, for so he **Ywain li** thought that none would know him. Lancelot **Aoutres** overtaketh him and crieth, 'By my head, Kay the Seneschal, shame had you enough of that you did to King Arthur when you slew his son, and as much more ought you now to have of thus warring upon him again!' He smiteth his horse of his spurs, lance in rest, and Kay the Seneschal turneth toward him, and they mell together with their spears on their shields, and pierce them in such sort that an ells-length of each shaft passeth through beyond.

XIV

The lances were strong so as that they brast not. They draw them back to themselves so stoutly and come together so fiercely that their horses stagger and they lose the stirrups. Lancelot catcheth Kay the Seneschal at the passing beyond, in the midst of the breast, and thrusteth his spear into him so far that the point remained in the flesh, and Kay to-brast his own; and sore grieved was he when he felt himself wounded. The knight that was wounded overthrew one of the two knights. Kay is on the ground, and Lancelot taketh his horse and setteth Messire Ywain li Aoutres thereupon, that was right sore wounded so as that he scarce might bear it. Kay the Seneschal maketh his knight remount, and holdeth his sword grasped in his fist as though he had been stark wood. Lancelot seeth the two knights sore badly wounded, and thinketh that and he stay longer

they may remain on the field. He maketh
them go before him, and Kay the Seneschal
followeth them behind, himself the third knight,
that is right wroth of the wound he feeleth and
the blood that he seeth. Lancelot bringeth off
his knights like as the wild-boar goeth among
the dogs, and Kay dealeth him great buffets of
his sword when he may catch him, and Lancelot him again, and so they depart, fencing in
such sort.

XV

When Kay the Seneschal seeth that he may
not harm him, he turneth him back, full of great
wrath, and his heart pricketh to avenge him
thereof and he may get at him, for he is the
knight of the court that most he hateth. He is
come back to the Castle of the Hard Rock.
Briant of the Isles asketh him who hath
wounded him in such sort, and he telleth him
that he was bringing thither Ywain li Aoutres
when Lancelot rescued him. 'And the King,'
saith Briant, 'Is he repaired thither?' 'I
have heard no tidings of him at all,' saith Kay,
'For no leisure had I to ask of any.' Briant
and his knights take much thought as concerning
Lancelot's coming, for they are well persuaded
that Lancelot hath come for that the King is
dead and Messire Gawain, whereof they make
right great joy. Kay the Seneschal maketh
him be disarmed and his wound searched.
They tell him he need not fear it shall be his
death, but that he is right sore wounded.

XVI

Lancelot is entered into the castle of Cardoil,
and his wounded knights withal, and findeth the
folk in sore dismay. Great dole make they in
many places and much lamentation for King
Arthur, and say that now nevermore may they
look for succour to none, and he be dead and
Messire Gawain. But they give Lancelot joy
of that he hath rescued Messire Ywain li
Aoutres, and were so somewhat comforted and
made great cheer. The tidings thereof came
to the knights that were in the castle, and they
all come forward to meet him save they that
were wounded, and so led him up to the castle,
and Messire Ywain with him and the other
knight that was wounded. All the knights of
the castle were right glad, and ask him tidings
of King Arthur, and whether he were dead or
no. And Lancelot telleth them that he was
departed from him at the Palace Meadow,
where he won the white destrier and the crown
of gold there where the tidings were brought
to him that Queen Guinievre was dead.

XVII

' Then you tell us of a truth that the King is
on live, and Messire Gawain?' 'Both, you
may be certain!' saith Lancelot. Thereupon
were they gladder than before. They told him
of their own mischance, how Briant of the Isles
had put them to the worse, and how Kay the
Seneschal was with him to do them hurt. For he
it is that taketh most pains to do them evil. ' By

my head,' saith Lancelot, 'Kay the Seneschal
ought of right to take heed and with-hold him
from doing you ill, but he departed from the
field with the point of my spear in him when I
rescued Messire Ywain.'

XVIII

The knights are much comforted of the
coming of Lancelot, but he is much grieved
that he findeth so many of them wounded.
Meliant of the Waste Manor is at the castle of
the Hard Rock, and good fellow is it betwixt
him and Kay the Seneschal. He is right glad
of the tidings he hath heard, that Lancelot is
come, and saith that he is the knight of the
world that most he hateth, and that he will
avenge him of his father and he may meet him.
There come before the castle of Cardoil one day
threescore knights armed, and they seize upon
their booty betwixt the castle and the forest.
Lancelot issueth forth, all armed, and seven of
the best of the castle with him. He cometh
upon them after that they have led away their
plunder. He overtaketh one knight and smiteth
him with his spear right through the body, and
the other knights make an onset upon the others
and many to-brake their spears, and much
clashing was there of steel on armour; and there
fell at the assembly on one side and the other
full a score knights, whereof some were wounded
right sore. Meliant of the Waste Manor espied
Lancelot, and right great joy made he of seeing
him, and smiteth him so stout a buffet on the
shield that he to-breaketh his spear.

XIX

Lancelot smiteth him amidst the breast so grimly that he maketh him bend backwards over the saddle behind, and so beareth him to the ground, legs uppermost, over his horse croup, and trampleth him under his horse's feet. Lancelot was minded to alight to the ground to take him, but Briant of the Isles cometh and maketh him mount again perforce. The numbers grew on the one side and the other of knights that came from Cardoil and from the Hard Rock. Right great was the frushing of lances and the clashing of swords and the overthrow of horses and knights. Briant of the Isles and Lancelot come against each other so stoutly that they pierce their shields and cleave their habergeons, and they thrust with their spears so that the flesh is broken under the ribs and the shafts are all-to-splintered. They hurtle against each other so grimly at the by-passing that their eyes sparkle as it were of stars in their heads, and the horses stagger under them. They hold their swords drawn, and so return the one toward the other like lions. Such buffets deal they upon their helms that they beat them in and make the fire leap out by the force of the smiting of iron by steel. And Meliant cometh all armed toward Lancelot to aid Briant of the Isles, but Lucan the Butler cometh to meet him, and smiteth him with his spear so stoutly that he thrusteth it right through his shield and twisteth his arm against his side. He breaketh his spear at the by-passing, and

Briant
and
Lancelot Meliant also breaketh his, but he was wounded passing sore.

XX

Thereupon he seizeth him by the bridle and thinketh to lead him away, but the knights and the force of Briant rescue him. The clashing of arms lasted great space betwixt Briant of the Isles and Lancelot, and each was mightily wrath for that each was wounded. Either seized other many times by the bridle, and each was right fain to lead the other to his own hold, but the force of knights on the one side and the other disparted them asunder. Thus the stour lasted until evening, until that the night sundered them. But Briant had nought to boast of at departing, for Lancelot and his men carried off four of his by force right sore wounded, besides them that remained dead on the field. Briant of the Isles and Meliant betook them back all sorrowful for their knights that are taken and dead. Lancelot cometh back to Cardoil, and they of the castle make him right great joy of the knights that they bring taken, and say that the coming of the good knight Lancelot should be great comfort to them until such time as King Arthur should repair back and Messire Gawain. The wounded knights that were in the castle turned to healing of their wounds, whereof was Lancelot right glad. They were as many as five and thirty within the castle. Of all the King's knights were there no more save Lancelot and the wounded knight that he brought along with him.

BRANCH XXV

TITLE I

HERE the story is silent of Lancelot and the knights that are at Cardoil, and saith that King Arthur and Messire Gawain are in the castle where the priest told Messire Gawain how he was born. But they cannot depart thence at their will, for Ahuret the Bastard that was brother of Nabigant of the Rock, that Messire Gawain slew on account of Meliot of Logres, knoweth well that they are therewithin, and hath assembled his knights and holdeth them within so strait that they may not depart without sore damage. For he hath on the outer side a full great plenty of knights, and the King and Messire Gawain have with them but only five of the forest and the country that are upon their side, and they hold them so strait within that they may not issue out from thence; yea, the brother of Nabigant sweareth that they shall not depart thence until such time as he shall have taken Messire Gawain, and taken vengeance on his fellow of his brother whom he slew. The King saith to Messire Gawain that he hath much shame of this that they are so long shut up therewithin, and that he better loveth to die with honour than to live with shame within the castle. So they issued forth, spears in rest, and Ahuret and his knights,

143

Ahuret the Bastard whereof was there great plenty, made much joy thereat.

II

The King and Messire Gawain strike among them, and each overthroweth his man; but Ahuret hath great shame of this that he seeth his knights put to the worse by so few folk. He setteth his spear in rest and smiteth one of King Arthur's knights through the body and beareth him down dead. Then returneth he to Messire Gawain, and buffeteth him so strongly that he pierceth his shield, but he maketh drop his own spear and loseth his stirrups, and Messire Gawain waxeth wroth and smiteth him so grimly and with such force that he maketh him bend back over the hinder bow of his saddle. But Ahuret was strong and of great might, and leapeth back between the bows and cometh toward King Arthur that he saw before him, but he knew him not. He left Messire Gawain, and the King smiteth him with such a sweep that he cutteth off his arm, spear and all. There was great force of knights, so that they ran upon them on all sides; and never would they have departed thence sound and whole, but that thereupon Meliot of Logres cometh thither with fifteen knights, for that he had heard tidings of Messire Gawain, how he was besieged in a castle there, where he and King Arthur between them were in such plight that they had lost their five knights, so that they were not but only two that defended themselves as best they might, as they that had no thought

but to remain there, for the odds of two knights **Meliot**
against thirty was too great. · **of Logres**

III

Thereupon, behold you, Meliot of Logres
with fifteen knights, and they come thither
where the King and Messire Gawain are in
such jeopardy, and they strike so stoutly among
them that they rescue King Arthur and Messire
Gawain from them that had taken them by the
bridle, and so slay full as many as ten of them,
and put the others to flight, and lead away their
lord sore maimed.   And Messire Gawain
giveth Meliot much thanks of the bounty he
hath done, whereby he hath saved them their
lives ; and he giveth him the castle, and is fain
that he hold it of him, for in no place might he
have better employment, and that well hath he
deserved it of his service in such need.   Meliot
thanketh him much, and prayeth Messire
Gawain instantly that and he shall have need
of succour he will come to aid him, in like
manner as he would do by him everywhere.
And Messire Gawain telleth him that as of this
needeth him not to make prayer, for that he is
one of the knights of the world that most he
ought of right to love.   The King and Messire
Gawain take leave of Meliot, and so depart,
and Meliot garnisheth the castle that was right
fair and rich and well-seated.

BRANCH XXVI

TITLE I

Arthur at
Avalon OF Meliot the story is here silent, and saith
that King Arthur and Messire Gawain
have ridden so far that they are come into the
Isle of Avalon, there where the Queen lieth.
They lodge the night with the hermits, that
make them right great cheer. But you may
well say that the King is no whit joyful when
he seeth the coffin where the Queen lieth and
that wherein the head of his son lieth. Thereof is his dole renewed, and he saith that this
holy place of this holy chapel ought he of right
to love better than all other places on earth.
They depart on the morrow when they have
heard mass. The King goeth the quickest
he may toward Cardoil, and findeth the land
wasted and desolate in many places, whereof is
he right sorrowful, and understandeth that Kay
the Seneschal warreth upon him with the others.
He marvelleth much how he durst do it. He
is come to Cardoil. When they of the castle
know it they come to meet him with right great
cheer. The tidings went throughout all the
land, and they of the country were right joyous
thereof, for the more part believed that he was
dead. They of the castle of the Hard Rock
knew it, but little rejoiced they thereat. But
Kay the Seneschal was whole of his wound and

bethought him that great folly would he do to remain longer there to war upon the King, for well knew he that and the King held him and did that which he had proclaimed, his end were come. He departeth from the castle, where he had sojourned of a long while, and crossed again stealthily over-sea, and came into Little Britain, and made fast a castle for fear of the King, that is called Chinon, and was there long time, without the King warring upon him, for enough adventures had he in other parts.

II

To Cardoil was the King repaired and Messire Gawain. You may well understand that the land was much rejoiced thereof, and that all the knights were greatly comforted, and knights came back to the court from all parts. They that had been wounded were whole again. Briant of the Isles stinted not of his pride nor of his outrage, but rather stirred up the war the most he might, he and Meliant still more, and said that never would he cease therefrom until death, nor never would he have rest until such time as he should have vengeance of Lancelot. The King was one day at Cardoil at meat, and there was in the hall great throng of knights, and Messire Gawain sate beside the King. Lancelot sate at the table, and Messire Ywain the son of King Urien, and Sagramors li Desirous, and Ywain li Aoutres, and many more other knights round about the table, but there were not so many as there wont to be. Messire Lucan the Butler

Made-
glant of
Oriande
served before the King of the golden cup. The King looked round about the table and remembered him of the Queen. He was bent upon thinking rather than on eating, and saw that his court was much wasted and worsened of her death. And what time the King was musing in such sort, behold you a knight come into the hall all armed before the King; and he leaneth on the staff of his spear. 'Sir,' saith the knight, 'Listen, so please you, to me, and all these others, listen! Madeglant of Oriande sendeth me here to you, and commandeth that you yield up the Table Round to him, for sith that the Queen is dead, you have no right thereof, for he is her next of kin and he that hath the best right to have and to hold it; and, so you do not this, you he defieth as the man that disheriteth him, for he is your enemy in two manner of ways, for the Table Round that you hold by wrong, and for the New Law that you hold. But he sendeth you word by me, that so you will renounce your belief and take Queen Jandree his sister, that he will cry you quit as of the Table Round and will be of your aid everywhere. But and if you do not this, have never affiance in him. And so sendeth he word to you by me!'

III

Therewith the knight departeth, and the King remaineth all heavy in thought, and when they had eaten, he rose from the tables and all the knights. He speaketh to Messire Gawain and Lancelot, and taketh counsel with all the others. 'Sir,' saith Messire Gawain, 'You Of King will defend yourself the best you may, and we Arthur will help you to smite your enemies. Great Britain is all at your will. You have not as yet lost any castle. Nought hath been broken down nor burnt but open ground and cottages and houses, whereof is no great harm done to yourself, and the shame thereof may lightly be amended. King Madeglant is of great hardiment as of words, but in arms will he not vanquish you so soon. If that he warreth upon you toward the West, send thither one of the best knights of your court that may maintain the war and defend the land against him.'

IV

The King sojourned at Cardoil of a long space. He believed in God and His sweet Mother right well. He brought thither from the castle where the Graal was the pattern whereby chalices should be made, and commanded make them throughout all the land so as that the Saviour of the world should be served more worshipfully. He commanded also that bells be cast throughout his land after the fashion of the one he had brought, and that each church should have one according to the means thereof. This much pleased the people of his kingdom, for thereby was the land somewhat amended. The tidings came to him one day that Briant and Meliant were riding through his land with great routs of folk, and were minded to assiege Pannenoisance; and the King issued forth of Cardoil with great throng of knights all armed, and rode until he espied Briant and his people, and Briant him again.   They ranged their battles on both sides, and came together with such might and so great a shock as that it seemed the earth shook; and they melled together at the assembly with their spears so passing grimly as that the frushing thereof might be heard right far away.   Some fourteen fell in the assembly that rose up again never more. Meliant of the Waste Manor searcheth for Lancelot in the midst of the stour until he findeth him, and runneth upon him right sturdily and pierceth his shield with his spear. Lancelot smiteth him such a sweep amidst the breast, that he thrusteth his spear right through his shoulder, and pinneth him so strongly that the shaft is all to-brast, and the end thereof remaineth in his body.   And Meliant, all stricken through as he is, runneth upon him and passeth his spear right through the shield and through the arm, in such sort that he pinneth it to his side.   He passeth beyond and breaketh his spear, and afterward returneth to Lancelot, sword in fist, and dealeth him a buffet on the helm so grimly that he all to-battered it in.   Lancelot waxeth right wroth thereof, and he grieveth the more for that he feeleth him wounded.   He cometh toward Meliant, sword drawn, and holding him well under cover of his shield and cover of his helm, and smiteth Meliant so fiercely that he cleaveth his shoulder down to the rib in such sort that the end of the spear wherewith he had pierced

him fell out therefrom.   Meliant felt himself **Briant**
wounded to the death, and draweth him back **sore hurt**
all sorrowful, and other knights run upon
Lancelot and deliver assault.   Messire Ywain
and Sagramors li Desirous and Messire Gawain
were on the other side in great jeopardy, for
the people of Briant of the Isles came from all
parts, and waxed more and more, and on all
sides the greater number of knights had the
upper hand therein.   King Arthur and Briant
of the Isles were in the midst of the battle, and
dealt each other right great buffets.   Briant's
people come thither and take King Arthur by
the bridle, and the King defendeth himself as a
good knight, and maketh a ring about him
amongst them that attack him, the same
as doth a wild boar amongst the dogs.
Messire Ywain is come thither and Lucan the
Butler, and break through the press by force.
Thereupon, behold you Sagramors li Desirous,
that cometh as fast as his horse may gallop
under him, and smiteth Briant of the Isles right
before his people with such a rush that he
beareth him to the ground in a heap, both him
and his horse.   Briant to-brast his thigh bone
in the fall that he made.   Sagramors holdeth
sword drawn and would fain have thrust it into
his body, when the King crieth to him that he
slay him not.

V

Briant's people were not able to succour their
lord.   Nay, rather, they drew back on all sides,
for the stour had lasted of a long space.   So

Meliant
dieth

they tended the dead and the wounded, of whom were enough on one side and the other. King Arthur made carry Briant of the Isles to Cardoil, and bring along the other knights that his own knights had taken. Right joyous were the folks at Cardoil when the King came back. They bore Meliant of the Waste Manor on his shield to the Hard Rock, but he scarce lived after. The King made Briant of the Isles be healed, and held him in prison of a long while, until Briant gave him surety of all his lands and became his man. The King made him Seneschal of all his lands, and Briant served him right well.

VI

Lancelot was whole of his wound, and all the knights of theirs. King Arthur was safely stablished, and redoubted and dreaded of all lands and of his own land like as he wont to be. Briant hath forgotten all that is past, and is obedient to the King's commands, and more privy is he of his counsel than ever another of the knights, insomuch that he put the others somewhat back, whereof had they much misliking. The felony of Kay the Seneschal lay very nigh the King's heart, and he said that and any would take vengeance upon him for the same, greatly would he love him thereof, for so disloyally hath he wrought against him that he durst not let the matter be slurred over ; and a sore misfortune is it for the world when a man of so poor estate hath slain so high a man as his son for no misdeed, and that strangers ought by

as good right as they that knew him or himself Queen
take vengeance upon him thereof, so that others Jandree
might be adread of doing such disloyalty.

VII

Briant was feared and redoubted throughout
all Great Britain.   King Arthur had told them
that they were all to be at his commandment.
And one day while the King was at Cardoil,
behold you! a damsel that cometh into the hall
and saith to him : 'Sir, Queen Jandree hath
sent me over to you, and biddeth you do that
whereof her brother sent you word by his
knight.   She is minded to be Lady and Queen
of your land, and that you take her to wife, for
of high lineage is she and of great power, wherefore she biddeth you by me that you renounce
the New Law and that you believe in the God
in whom she believeth, and, so you do not this,
you may not have affiance in your land, for
King Madeglant hath as now made ready his
host to enter into the chief of your land, and
hath sworn his oath that he will not end until
he shall have passed all the borders of the isles
that march upon your land, and shall come upon
Great Britain with all his strength, and so seize
the Table Round that ought to be his own
of right.   And my Lady herself would come
hither but for one thing, to wit, that she hath in
her such disdain of them that believe in the
New Law, that she deigneth not behold none of
them, for, so soon as she was stablished Queen,
made she her eyes be covered for that she would
not look upon none that were of that believe.

Jandree's But the Gods wherein she believeth did so
message much for her, for that she loveth and worship-
peth them, that she may discover her eyes and
her face, and yet see not at all, whereof is she right
glad, for that the eyes in her head are beautiful
and gentle. But great affiance hath she in her
brother, that is mighty and puissant, for he hath
her in covenant that he will destroy all them
that believe in the New Law, in all places
where he may get at them, and, when he shall
have destroyed them in Great Britain and the
other islands, so that my Lady might not see
none therein, so well is she with the Gods
wherein she believeth, that she will have her
sight again all whole, nor until that hour is
she fain to see nought.'

VIII

'Damsel,' saith the King, 'I have heard
well that which you tell me of this that you
have in charge to say; but tell your Lady on
my behalf, that the Law which the Saviour
of the world hath established by His death and
by His crucifixion never will I renounce, for the
love that I have in Him. But tell her that she
believe in God and in His sweet Mother, and
that she believe in the New Law, for by the
false believe wherein she abideth is she blinded
in such sort, nor never will she see clear until
she believe in God. Tell her moreover, I send
her word that never more shall there be Queen
in my land save she be of like worth as was
Queen Guenievre.' 'Then I tell you plainly,'
saith she, 'that you will have betimes such

tidings as that good for you they will not be.' **of**
The damsel departeth from Cardoil, and cometh **defiance**
back to where the Queen was, and telleth her
the message King Arthur sendeth her. 'True,'
saith she, 'I love him better than all in the
world, and yet refuseth he my will and my
commandment. Now may he no longer endure!' She sendeth to her brother King
Madeglant, and telleth him that she herself doth
defy him and he take not vengeance on King
Arthur and bring him not into prison.

TITLE I

King
Made-
glant

THIS history saith that the land of this King was full far away from the land of King Arthur, and that needs must he pass two seas or ever he should approach the first head of King Arthur's land. He arrived in Albanie with great force of men with a great navy. When they of the land knew it, they garnished them against him and defended their lands the best they might; then they sent word to King Arthur that King Madeglant was come in such manner into the land, with great plenty of folk, and that he should come presently to succour them or send them a knight so good as that he might protect them, and that in case he doth not so, the land will be lost. When King Arthur understood these tidings, it was not well with him. He asked his knights whom he might send thither. And they say, let him send Lancelot thither, for that he is a worthy knight and a kingly, and much understandeth of war, and hath in him as much loyalty as hath ever another that they know. The King maketh him come before him.

II

'Lancelot,' saith the King, 'Such affiance have I in you and in your knighthood, that it is

my will to send you to the furthest corner of my **Lancelot**
land, to protect it, with the approval of my **goeth**
knights, wherefore I pray and require you that **forth**
you do your power herein as many a time have
you done already in my service. And I will
give you in command forty knights.' 'Sir,'
saith Lancelot, 'Against your will am I not
minded to be, but in your court are there other
knights full as good, or better than I, whom
you might well send thither. But I would not
that you should hold this of cowardize in me,
and right willingly will I do your pleasure, for
none ought I to serve more willingly than you.'
The King giveth him much thanks of this that
he saith. Lancelot departeth from the court, and
taketh forty knights with him, and so cometh
into the land of Albanie where King Madeglant
hath arrived. When they of the land knew
that Lancelot was come, great joy had they
thereof in their hearts, for ofttimes had they
heard tell of him and of his good knighthood.
They were all at his commandment, and received
him as their champion and protector.

III

King Madeglant one day issued forth of his
ships to do battle against Lancelot and them of
the land. Lancelot received him right stoutly,
and slew many of his folk, and the more part
fled and would fain have drawn them to their
ships, but Lancelot and his people went after
and cut a part of them to pieces. King
Madeglant, with as many of his men as he
might, betaketh himself to his own ship privily,

and maketh put to sea the soonest he may.
They that might not come to the ships remained
on dry land, and were so cut up and slain.
Madeglant went his way discomfited. Of ten
ships full of men that he had brought he took
back with him but two. The land was in peace
and assured in safety. Lancelot remained there
of a long space. They of the country loved
him much and gave themselves great joy of
his valour and his great bounty, insomuch that
most of them say ofttimes that they would fain
have such a knight as was he for king, by the
goodwill of King Arthur, for that the land is
too far away; but and if he would set there a
knight or other man that might protect the
land, they would take it in right good part, and
he should hold the land of him, for they might
not safeguard it at their will without a champion,
for that land without a lord may but little avail.
They of the land loved Lancelot well, as I tell
you. King Arthur was at Cardoil, and so were
his knights together with him. He thought to
be assured in his kingdom and to live peaceably;
but what time he sate at meat one day in
Cardoil, behold you thereupon a knight that
cometh before the Table Round without saluting
him. 'Sir,' saith he, 'Where is Lancelot?'
'Sir,' saith the King to the knight, 'He is not
in this country.' 'By my head,' saith the
knight, 'that misliketh me. Wheresoever he
be, he is your knight and of your household;
wherefore King Claudas sendeth you word that
he is his mortal enemy, and you also, if so
be that for love of him you receive him from

this day forward, for he hath slain his sister's *Claudas*
son, Meliant of the Waste Manor, and he slew *defieth*
the father of Meliant likewise, but the father *Arthur*
belongeth not to King Claudas.

IV

'Meliant was the son of his sister-german,
wherefore much grieveth he of his death.'
'Sir knight,' saith the King, 'I know not
how the covenant may be between them as of
this that you tell me, but well know I that
King Claudas holdeth many a castle that King
Claudas ought not of right to have, whereof he
disherited his father, but meet is it that each
should conquer his own right. But so much I
tell you plainly, that never will I fail mine own
knight and he be such as durst defend himself
of murder, but and if he hath no will to do
this, then well may I allow that right be done
upon him. But, sith that he will not love his
own death, neither I nor other ought greatly to
love him and he refuse to redress his wrong.
When Lancelot shall know these tidings, I
know well that such is his valour and his
loyalty that he will readily answer in reason,
and will do all that he ought to do to clear
himself of such a charge.' 'Sir,' saith the
knight, 'You have heard well that I have told
you. Once more, I tell you plainly, King
Claudas sendeth you word that so you harbour
his enemy henceforward and in such manner as
you have done heretofore, he will be less than
pleased with you.'

V

With that the knight departeth, and the King remaineth at Cardoil. He sendeth for Briant of the Isles, his seneschal, and a great part of his knights, and demandeth counsel of them what he may do. Messire Ywain saith that he killed Meliant in the King's service, as one that warred upon his land, albeit the King had done him no wrong, and had so made common cause with the King's enemies without demanding right in his court. Nor never had Meliant appealed Lancelot of murder nor of treason, nor required him of the death of his father. Rather, Lancelot slew him in open war, as one that warred upon his lord by wrong. Sir,' saith Messire Ywain to the King, 'Howsoever Lancelot might have wrought in respect of Meliant, your land ought not to be called to account, for you were not in the kingdom, nor knew not that either had done other any wrong, and therefore say I that King Claudas will do great wrong and he bring plaint or levy war against you on this account.' 'Messire Ywain,' saith Briant of the Isles, 'matter of common knowledge is it that Lancelot slew the lord of the Waste Manor and Meliant his son after the contention that was betwixt King Arthur and me. But, after that he had slain the father, he ought of right to have taken good heed that he did no wrong to the son, but rather ought he to have sought peace and accord.'

VI

'Briant,' saith Messire Gawain, 'Lancelot is not here; and, moreover, he is now on the King's business. Well know you that Meliant came to you and that you made him knight, and that thereafter he warred upon the King's land without reasonable occasion. The King was far away from the land as he that made pilgrimage to the Graal. He was told tidings that his land was being put to the worse, and he sent Lancelot to protect it. He accordingly maintained the war as best he might until such time as the King was returned. Meliant knew well that the King was come back, and that never had he done wrong to none in his court that wished to demand right therein. He neither came thither nor sent, either to do right or to demand right, whether he did so for despite or whether it was for that he knew not how to do it. In the meanwhile he warred upon the King, that had never done him a wrong nor refused to do him a right. Lancelot slew him in the King's war and upon his land in defence thereof. There was peace of the war, as was agreed on between you and the King, but and if any should therefore hold Lancelot to blame of the death of Meliant, meseemeth that therein is he wrong. For the others are not held to answer for them that they slew; but and if you wish to say that Lancelot hath not slain him with reason, howsoever he may have wrought aforetime in respect of his father, I am ready to maintain his right by my body on behalf of his.'

VII

'Messire Gawain,' saith Briant of the Isles,
'You will not as at this time find none that
will take up your gage on account of this affair,
nor ought any to make enemies of his friends,
nor ought you to counsel me so to do.   King
Madeglant warreth upon him and King Claudas
maketh war upon him also.   They will deliver
attacks enough.   But I should well allow, for
the sake of saving his land and keeping his
friends, that the King should suffer Lancelot to
remain at a distance from his court for one
year, until tidings should have come to King
Claudas that he had been bidden leave thereof,
so as that King Arthur might have his good
will and his love.'   Sagramors li Desirous
leapeth forward.   'Briant of the Isles,' saith
Sagramors, 'Ill befall him that shall give such
counsel to a lord of his knight, and the knight
have well served his lord, albeit he may have
slain in his wars a knight without murder and
without treason, that he should give him his
leave!   Right ill will Lancelot hitherto have
bestowed his services, and the King on this
account give him his leave!   After that, let
King Claudas come!   Let him lay waste and
slay, and right great worship shall King Arthur
have thereof!   I say not this for that Lancelot
hath need be afeared of King Claudas body to
body, nor of the best knight in his land, but
many things befall whereof one taketh no heed;
and so King Arthur give leave to Lancelot
from his court, it will be counted unto him for

cowardize, and neither I nor you nor other **Angry** knight ought never more to have affiance in **words** him.' 'Lord,' saith Briant of the Isles, 'Better would it avail the King to give Lancelot leave for one year, than it would to fight for him ten years and have his land wasted and put to the worse.'

VIII

Thereupon, behold you! Orguelleux of the Launde come, that had not been at the court of a long time, and it had been told him whereof these words were. 'Briant,' saith Orguelleux of the Launde, 'Evil fare the knight that would fain grieve and harm with their lord them that have served him well! Sith that Lancelot is not here, say nought of him that ought not to be said. The court of King Arthur hath been as much renowned and made honoured by Lancelot as by ever another knight that is in it, and, but for him, never would his court have been so redoubted as it is. For no knight is there so cruel to his foes nor so redoubted throughout all Great Britain as is Lancelot, and, for that King Arthur loveth you, make him not that he hate his knights, for such four or such six be there in his castle as may depart therefrom without returning, the loss whereof should scarce be made good by us. Lancelot hath well served the King aforetime, and the King well knoweth how much he is worth; and if so be that King Claudas purposeth to war on King Arthur for Lancelot's sake, according as I have heard,

Orguel-
leux his
counsel
without any reason, and King Arthur be not more craven than he wont to be, he may well abide his warfare and his strife so treason harm him not. For so many good knights hath King Arthur yet, that none knoweth such knights nor such King in the world beside.'

BRANCH XXVIII

TITLE I

THIS story saith that Briant would have been wroth with a will against Orguelleux of the Launde, had it not been for the King, and Orguelleux against him, for Orguelleux heeded no danger when anger and ill-will carried him away. Therewithal the talk came to an end. When the King learnt the tidings that Madeglant was discomfited and that the land of Albanie was in peace, he sent word to Lancelot to return back. They of the land were very sorrowful when he departed, for great affiance had they in his chivalry. So he came back thither where King Arthur was. All they of the land made great joy, for well loved was he of many, nor were there none that hated him save of envy alone. They told him the tidings of King Claudas, and also in what manner Briant had spoken. Lancelot took no notice outwardly, as he that well knew how to redress all his grievances. He was at the court of a long while, for that King Claudas was about to send over thither some one of his knights. Briant of the Isles would fain that the King should have given him his leave, for more he hated him than ever another knight in the court, sith he it was that many a time had harmed him more than any other. By Briant's counsel, King Claudas sent

**Briant is
defeated** his knight to King Arthur's court, wherein did
he not wisely, for that he thereby renewed
a matter whereof afterward came right great
mischief, as this title witnesseth.

II

Madeglant of Oriande heard say that Lancelot
was repaired back, and that the land of Albanie
was all void save for the folk of the country.
He maketh ready his navy at once and cometh
back to the land in great force. He burneth
the land and layeth it waste on every side, and
doth far worse therein than he did aforetime.
They of the land sent over to King Arthur and
told him of their evil plight, warning him that,
and he send them not succour betimes, they will
leave the land and yield up the castles, for that
they might not hold them longer. He took
counsel, the King with his knights, whom he
might send thither, and they said that Lancelot
had already been there and that now another
knight should be sent thither. The King sent
thither Briant of the Isles, and lent him forty
knights. Briant, that loved not the King in his
heart, came into the land, but only made pretence
of helping him to defend it. One day fell out a
battle betwixt Madeglant and Briant and all their
men. Briant was discomfited, and had many of
his knights killed. Madeglant and his people
spread themselves over the land and laid the
towns in ruins and destroyed the castles, that
were disgarnished, and put to death all them
that would not believe in their gods, and cut off
their heads.

III

All they of the land and country longed
with sorrow for Lancelot, and said that had he
remained there, the land would not have been
thus destroyed, nor might they never have protection of no knight but of him alone.   Briant
of the Isles returned back, as he that would the
war against King Arthur should increase on
every side, for, what good soever the King may
do him, he loveth him not, nor never will so
long as he is on live.   But no semblant thereof
durst he show, for, sith that the best of his
knights had been slain in the battle, so had he
no power on his side, as against Lancelot and
the good knights of his fellowship, whereof he
would fain that there had been not one.

IV

King Arthur was at Cardoil on one day of
Whitsuntide.   Many were the knights that
were come to this court whereof I tell you.
The King was seated at meat, and the day was
fair and clear, and the air clean and fresh.
Sagramors li Desirous and Lucan the Butler
served before the King.   And what time they
had served of the first meats, therewithal behold
you, a quarrel, like as it had been shot from a
cross-bow, and striketh in the column of the
hall before the King so passing strong that there
was not a knight in the hall but heard it when
it struck therein.   They all looked thereat in
great wonderment.   The quarrel was like as
it were of gold, and it had about it a many costly

precious stones. The King saith that quarrel
so costly cometh not from a poor place.
Lancelot and Messire Gawain say that never
have they seen one so rich. It struck so deep
in the column that the iron point thereof might
not be seen, and a good part of the shaft was
also hidden. Thereupon, behold you, a damsel
of surpassing great beauty that cometh, sitting on
a right costly mule, full well caparisoned. She
had a gilded bridle and gilded saddle, and was
clad in a right rich cloth of silk. A squire
followed after her that drove her mule from
behind. She came before King Arthur as
straight as she might, and saluted him right
worshipfully, and he made answer the best he
might. 'Sir,' saith she, 'I am come to speak
and demand a boon, nor will I never alight
until such time as you shall have granted it to
me. For such is my custom, and for this am
I come to your court, whereof I have heard
such tidings and such witness in many places
where I have been, that I know you will not
deny me herein.'

V

'Damsel, tell me what boon you would have
of me?' 'Sir,' saith she, 'I would fain pray
and beseech you that you bid the knight that
may draw forth this quarrel from this column
go thither where there is sore need of him.'
'Damsel,' saith the King, 'Tell me the need.'
'Sir,' saith she, 'I will tell it you plainly when
I shall see the knight that shall have drawn it
forth.' 'Damsel,' saith the King, 'Alight!

Never, please God, shall you go forth of my **Excuses**
court denied of that you ask.' Lucan the Butler **pleaded**
taketh her between his arms and setteth her to
the ground, and her mule is led away to be
stabled. When the damsel had washen, she
was set in a seat beside Messire Ywain, that
showed her much honour and served her with
a good will. He looked at her from time to
time, for she was fair and gentle and of good
countenance. When they had eaten at the
tables, the damsel prayeth the King that he
will hasten them to do her business. 'Sir,' saith
she, 'Many a good knight is there within
yonder, and right glad may he be that shall
draw it forth, for I tell you a right good knight
is he, sith that none may achieve this business
save he alone.' 'Fair nephew,' saith the
King, 'Now set your hand to this quarrel and
give it back to the damsel.' 'Ha, sir,' saith
he, 'Do me not shame! By the faith that I
owe you, I will not set my hand forward
herein this day, nor ought you to be wroth
hereof. Behold, here have you Lancelot with
you, and so many other good knights, that little
worship should I have herein were I to set
myself forward before them.' 'Messire Ywain,'
saith the King, 'Set your hand hereto! It
may be that you think too humbly of yourself
herein.' 'Sir,' saith Messire Ywain, 'Nought
is there in the world that I would not do
for you, but as for this matter I pray you
hold me excused.' 'Sagramors, and you,
Orguelleux of the Launde, what will you
do?' saith the King. 'Sir,' say they, 'When

Lancelot hath made assay, we will do your pleasure, but before him, so please you, we will not go.'

VI

'Damsel,' saith the King, 'Pray Lancelot that he be fain to set his hand, and then the rest shall go after him if needs be.' 'Lancelot,' saith the damsel, 'By the thing that most you love, make not mine errand bootless, but set your hand to the quarrel and then will the others do that they ought of right to do. For no leisure have I to tarry here long time.' 'Damsel,' saith Lancelot, 'Ill do you, and a sin, to conjure me for nought, for so many good knights be here within, that I should be held for a fool and a braggart and I put myself forward before all other.' 'By my head,' saith the King, 'Not so! Rather will you be held as a knight courteous and wise and good, as now you ought to be, and great worship will it be to yourself and you may draw forth the quarrel, and great courtesy will it be to aid the damsel. Wherefore I require you, of the faith you owe me, that you set your hand thereto, sith that the damsel prayeth you so to do, before the others.'

VII

Lancelot hath no mind to disobey the King's commandment; and he remembered that the damsel had conjured him by the thing that most he loved; nor was there nought in the world that he loved so much as the Queen, albeit she was dead, nor never thought he of The none other thing save her alone. Then standeth Chapel he straight upright, doth off his robe, and cometh Perilous straight to the quarrel that is fixed in the column. He setteth his hand thereunto and draweth it forth with a right passing strong wrench, so sturdily that he maketh the column tremble. Then he giveth it to the damsel. 'Sir,' saith she to King Arthur, 'Now is it my devoir to tell you plainly of my errand; nor might none of the knights here within have drawn forth the quarrel save only he; and you held me in covenant how he that should draw it forth should do that which I shall require of him, and that he might do it, nor will I pray nor require of him nought that is not reason. Needs must he go to the Chapel Perilous the swiftest he may, and there will he find a knight that lieth shrouded in the midst of the chapel: He will take of the cloth wherein he is shrouded and a sword that lieth at his side in the coffin, and will take them to the Castle Perilous; and when he shall there have been, he shall return to the castle where he slew the lion in the cavern wherein are the two griffons, and the head of one of them shall he take and bring to me at Castle Perilous, for a knight there lieth sick that may not otherwise be healed.'

VIII

'Damsel,' saith Lancelot, 'I see that you reckon but little of my life, so only that your wish be accomplished.' 'Sir,' saith she, 'I

Lancelot goeth forth know as well as you what the enterprise is, nor do I no whit desire your death, for, and were you dead, never would the knight be whole for whose sake you undertake it. And you will see the fairest damsel that is in any kingdom, and the one that most desireth to see you. And, so you tarry not, through her shall you lightly get done that you have to do. See now that you delay it not, but do that is needful swiftly sith that it hath been laid upon you, for the longer you tarry, the greater will be the hazard of mischance befalling you.' The damsel departeth from the court and taketh her leave and goeth her way back as fast as she may, and saith to herself: 'Lancelot, albeit you have these pains and this travail for me, yet would I not your death herein, but of right ought I to rejoice in your tribulation, for into two of the most perilous places in the world are you going. Greatly ought I to hate you, for you reft me of my friend and gave him to another, and while I live may I never forget it.' The damsel goeth her way, and Lancelot departeth from the court and taketh leave of the King and of all the others. He issueth forth of Cardoil, all armed, and entereth into the forest that is deep, and so goeth forth a great pace, and prayeth God guide him into safety.

THEREWITHAL the story is silent of Arthur Lancelot, and saith that Briant of the and Isles is repaired to Cardoil. Of the forty Briant knights that he took with him, but fifteen doth he bring back again. Thereof is King Arthur right sorrowful, and saith that he hath the fewer friends. They of the land of Albanie have sent to King Arthur and told him that and he would not lose the land for evermore he must send them Lancelot, for never saw they knight that better knew how to avenge him on his enemies and to do them hurt than was he. The King asketh Briant of the Isles how it is that his knights are dead in such sort? 'Sir,' saith Briant, 'Madeglant hath great force of people, and what force of men soever may run upon them, they make a castle of their navy in such sort that none may endure against them, and never did no folk know so much of war as do they. The land lieth far away from you, and more will it cost you to hold it than it is worth ; and, if you will believe my counsel, you will trouble yourself no more about it, and they of the country would be well counselled and they did the same.' 'Briant,' saith the King, 'This would be great blame to myself. No worshipful man ought to be idle in guarding and holding that which is his own. The worshipful man ought not to hold of things so much for their value as for their honour, and if I should leave the land disgarnished of my aid and my counsel, they will take mine, and will say that I have not heart to protect my land; and even now is it great shame to myself that they have settled themselves there and would fain draw away them of the land to their evil law. And I would fain that Lancelot had achieved that he hath undertaken, and I would have sent him there, for none would protect the land better than he, and, were he now there along with forty knights and with them of the country, Madeglant would make but short stay there.' 'Sir,' saith Briant, 'They of the country reckon nought of you nor any other but Lancelot only, and they say that and you send him there they will make him King.' 'It may well be that they say so,' saith the King, 'But never would Lancelot do aught that should be against my will.' 'Sir,' saith Briant, 'Sith that you are not minded to believe me, I will say no more in this matter, but in the end his knighthood will harm you rather than help you and you take no better heed thereof than up to this time you have done.'

BRANCH XXX

TITLE I

OF Briant of the Isles the story is here silent, whom the King believeth too much in many things, and saith that Lancelot goeth his way right through the forest, full heavy in thought. He had not ridden far when he met a knight that was right sore wounded. He asked him whence he came and who had wounded him in such manner. 'Sir,' saith he, 'I come from the Chapel Perilous, where I was not able to defend me against an evil folk that appeared there; and they have wounded me in such sort as you see, and but for a damsel that came thereinto from the forest I should not have escaped on live. But she aided me on such condition that and I should see a knight they call Lancelot, or Perceval, or Messire Gawain, I should tell which of them soever I should first meet withal that he should go to her without delay, for much she marvelleth her that none of them cometh into the chapel, for none ought to enter there but good knights only. But much do I marvel, Sir, how the damsel durst enter there, for it is the most marvellous place that is, and the damsel is of right great beauty; natheless she cometh thither oftentimes alone into the chapel. A knight lieth in the chapel that hath been slain of late, that was a fell and cruel

175

Meliot lieth sore wounded knight and a hardy.' 'What was his name?' saith Lancelot. 'He was named Ahuret the Bastard,' saith the knight; 'And he had but one arm and one hand, and the other was smitten off at a castle that Messire Gawain gave Meliot of Logres when he succoured him against this knight that lieth in the coffin. And Meliot of Logres hath slain the knight that had assieged the castle, but the knight wounded him sore, so that he may not be whole save he have the sword wherewith he wounded him, that lieth in the coffin at his side, and some of the cloth wherein he is enshrouded; and, so God grant me to meet one of the knights, gladly will I convey to him the damsel's message.' 'Sir Knight,' saith Lancelot, 'One of them have you found. My name is Lancelot, and for that I see you are wounded and in evil plight, I tell it you thus freely.' 'Sir,' saith the knight, 'Now may God protect your body, for you go in great peril of death. But the damsel much desireth to see you, I know not for what, and well may she aid you if she will.'

II

'Sir Knight, God hath brought us forth of many a peril, and so will He also from this and it be His pleasure and His will.' With that, Lancelot departeth from the knight, and hath ridden so far that he is come at evensong to the Chapel Perilous, that standeth in a great valley of the forest, and hath a little church-yard about it that is well enclosed on all sides, and hath an

ancient cross without the entrance.   The chapel **Lancelot**
and the grave-yard are overshadowed of the **in the**
forest, that is right tall.   Lancelot entereth **chapel**
therein all armed.   He signeth him of the
cross and blesseth him and commendeth him to
God.   He seeth in the grave-yard coffins in
many places, and it seemeth him that he seeth
folk round about that talk together, the one with
another.   But he might not hear that they said.
He might not see them openly, but very tall
they seemed him to be.   He is come toward
the chapel and alighteth of his horse, and seeth
a shed outside the chapel, wherein was pro-
vender for horses.   He goeth thither to set his
own there, then leaneth his shield against his
spear at the entrance of the chapel, and entereth
in, where it was very dark, for no light was
there save only of a single lamp that shone full
darkly.   He seeth the coffin that was in the
midst of the chapel wherein the knight lay.

III

When he had made his orison before an
image of Our Lady, he cometh to the coffin
and openeth it as fast as he may, and seeth the
knight, tall and foul of favour, that therein lay
dead.   The cloth wherein he was enshrouded
was displayed all bloody.   He taketh the sword
that lay at his side and lifteth the winding-
sheet to rend it at the seam, then taketh the
knight by the head to lift him upward, and
findeth him so heavy and so ungain that scarce
may he remove him.   He cutteth off the half
of the cloth wherein he is enshrouded, and the

coffin beginneth to make a crashing so passing
loud that it seemed the chapel were falling.
When he hath the piece of the cloth and the
sword he closeth the coffin again, and forthwith cometh to the door of the chapel and seeth
mount, in the midst of the grave-yard as it
seemed him, great knights and horrible, and
they are apparelled as it were to combat, and
him thinketh that they are watching for him
and espy him.

IV

Thereupon, behold you, a damsel running, her
kirtle girt high about her, right through the
grave-yard a great pace. 'Take heed you move
not until such time as it is known who the
knight is!' She is come to the chapel. 'Sir
Knight, lay down the sword and this that you
have taken of the winding-sheet of the dead
knight!' 'Damsel,' saith Lancelot, 'What
hurt doth it you of this that I have?' 'This,'
saith she, 'That you have taken it without my
leave; for I have him in charge, both him and
the chapel. And I would fain,' saith she,
'know what is your name?' 'Damsel,' saith
he, 'What would you gain of knowing my
name?' 'I know not,' saith she, 'whether I
shall have either loss or gain thereof, but high
time already is it that I should ask you it to my
sorrow, for many a time have I been deceived
therein.' 'Damsel,' saith he, 'I am called
Lancelot of the Lake.' 'You ought of right,'
saith she, 'to have the sword and the cloth;
but come you with me to my castle, for often-

times have I desired that you and Perceval and
Messire Gawain should see the three tombs
that I have made for your three selves.'

V

'Damsel,' saith he, 'No wish have I to see
my sepulchre so early betimes.' 'By my head,'
saith she, 'And you come not thither, you may
not issue from hence without tribulation; and
they that you see there are earthly fiends that
guard this grave-yard and are at my commandment.' 'Never, damsel, please God,' saith
Lancelot, 'may your devils have power to harm
a Christian.' 'Ha, Lancelot,' saith she, 'I
beseech and pray you that you come with me
into my castle, and I will save your life as at
this time from this folk that are just now ready
to fall upon you; and, so you are not willing to
do this, yield me back the sword that you have
taken from the coffin, and go your way at once.'
'Damsel,' saith Lancelot, 'Into your castle
may I not go, nor desire I to go, wherefore
pray me no more thereof, for other business
have I to do; nor will I yield you back the
sword, whatsoever may befall me, for a certain
knight may not otherwise be healed, and great
pity it were that he should die.' 'Ha, Lancelot,'
saith she, 'How hard and cruel do I find you
towards me! And as good cause have I to be
sorry that you have the sword as have you to
be glad. For, and you had not had it upon
you, never should you have carried it off from
hence at your will; rather should I have had all
my pleasure of you, and I would have made you

Lancelot be borne into my castle, from whence never
benighted should you have moved again for nought you
might do; and thus should I have been quit
of the wardenship of this chapel and of coming
thereinto in such manner as now oftentimes I
needs must come.

VI

'But now am I taken in a trap, for, so long
as you have the sword, not one of them that are
there yonder can do you evil nor hinder you
of going.' Of this was Lancelot not sorry.
He taketh leave of the damsel, that departeth
grudgingly, garnisheth him again of his arms,
then mounteth again on his horse and goeth his
way right through the grave-yard. He beholdeth
this evil folk, that were so foul and huge and
hideous, it seemed as if they would devour
everything. They made way for Lancelot, and
had no power to hurt him. He is issued forth
of the grave-yard and goeth his way through the
forest until daylight appeared about him, fair
and clear. He found the hermit there where
he had heard mass, then ate a little, then departed and rode the day long until setting of
the sun, but could find no hold on the one side
nor the other wherein he might lodge, and so
was benighted in the forest.

VII

Lancelot knew not which way to turn, for he
had not often been in the forest, and knew not
how the land lay nor the paths therein. He
rode until he found a little causeway, and there

was a path at the side that led to an orchard The
that was at a corner of the forest, where there Castle of
was a postern gate whereby one entered, and Griffons
it was not made fast for the night. And the
orchard was well enclosed with walls. Lancelot
entered in and made fast the entrance, then took
off his horse's bridle and let him feed on the
grass. He might not espy the castle that was
hard by for the abundance of trees and the
darkness of the night, and so knew not whither
he was arrived. He laid his shield for a pillow
and his arms at his side and fell on sleep. But,
had he known where it was he had come, little
sleep would he have had, for he was close to
the cavern where he slew the lion and where the
griffons were, that had come in from the forest
all gorged of victual, and were fallen on sleep,
and it was for them that the postern gate had
been left unbolted. A damsel went down from
a chamber by a trap-door with a brachet on her
arm for fear of the griffons, and as she went
toward the postern-gate to lock it, she espied
Lancelot, that lay asleep in the midst of the
orchard. She ran back to her Lady the
speediest she might, and said to her: 'Up,
Lady!' saith she, 'Lancelot is sleeping in the
orchard!' She leapt up incontinent and came
to the orchard there where Lancelot was sleeping, then sate her down beside him and began
to look at him, sighing the while, and draweth
as near him as she may. 'Fair Lord God,' saith
she, 'what shall I do? and I wake him first
he will have no care to kiss me, and if I kiss
him sleeping he will awake forthwith; and better

hap is it for me to take the most I may even in
such-wise than to fail of all, and moreover, if so
be I shall have kissed him, I may hope that
he will not hate me thereof, sith that I may
then boast that I have had at least so much
of that which is his own.' She set her mouth
close to him and so kissed him the best and
fairest she might, three times, and Lancelot
awakened forthwith. He leapt up and made
the cross upon him, then looked at the damsel,
and said: 'Ha, God! where, then, am I?'
'Fair sweet friend,' saith she, 'You are nigh
her that hath all set her heart upon you and will
remove it never.' 'I cry you mercy, damsel,'
saith Lancelot, 'and I tell you, for nought that
may befall, one that loveth me, please God,
never will I hate! but that which one hath
loved long time ought not so soon to fall away
from the remembrance of a love that is rooted
in the heart, when she hath been proven good
and loyal, nor ought one so soon to depart
therefrom.'

VIII

'Sir,' saith she, 'This castle is at your
commandment, and you will remain therein, and
well may you know my thought towards you.
Would that your thought were the same towards
me.' 'Damsel,' saith he, 'I seek the healing
of a knight that may not be healed save I bring
him the head of one of your serpents.' 'Certes,
Sir, so hath it been said. But I bade the
damsel say so only for that I was fain you
should come back hither to me.' 'Damsel,'

saith he, 'I have come back hither, and so may **The**
I turn back again sith that of the serpent's head **damsel**
is there no need.' 'Ha, Lancelot,' saith she, **plaineth**
'How good a knight are you, and how ill default
do you make in another way! No knight,
methinketh, is there in the world that would
have refused me save only you. This cometh
of your folly, and your outrage, and your
baseness of heart! The griffons have not done
my will in that they have not slain you or
strangled you as you slept, and, so I thought
that they would have power to slay you, I
would make them come to slay you now. But
the devil hath put so much knighthood into you
that scarce any man may have protection against
you. Better ought I to love you dead than
alive. By my head, I would fain that your
head were hanged with the others that hang
at the entrance of the gateway, and, had I
thought you would have failed me in such wise
I would have brought my father here to where
you were sleeping, and right gladly would he
have slain you.

IX

'None that knoweth the covenant between
me and you ought to hold you for a good
knight; for you have cozened me of my right
according to the tenor and custom of the castle
if that through perversity or slothfulness you
durst not take me when you have won me.'
'Damsel,' saith Lancelot, 'You may say your
will. You have done so much for me sithence
that I came hither that I ought not to be afeard

Castle of you, for traitor is the man or woman that
Perilous kisseth another to procure his hurt.' 'Lancelot,
I took but that I might have, for well I see
that none more thereof may I have never again.'
He goeth to put the bridle on his destrier, and
then taketh leave of the damsel, that parteth
from him right sorrowfully; but Lancelot would
no longer tarry, for great throng of knights was
there in the castle, and he was not minded to put
him in jeopardy for nought. He issueth forth
of the orchard, and the damsel looketh after
him as long as she may see him. After that,
cometh she to her chamber, sad and vexed at
heart, nor knoweth she how she may bear
herself, for the thing in the world that most she
loveth is far away, and no joy may she have
thereof.

x

Lancelot rideth right amidst the forest until
it is day, and cometh at the right hour of noon
to the Castle Perilous, where Meliot of Logres
lay. He entered into the castle. The damsel
that was at King Arthur's court cometh to
meet him. 'Lancelot,' saith she, 'Welcome
may you be!' 'Damsel,' saith he, 'Good
adventure may you have!' He was alighted
at the mounting-stage of the hall. She maketh
him mount up the steps and afterward be disarmed. 'Damsel,' saith he, 'Behold, here is
some of the winding-sheet wherein the knight
was shrouded, and here is his sword; but you
befooled me as concerning the serpent's head.'
'By my head,' saith the damsel, 'that did I

for the sake of the damsel of the Castle of
Griffons that hateth you not a whit, for so
prayed she me to do.   Now hath she seen you,
and so will she be more at ease, and will have
no cause to ask me thereof.'

XI

The damsel leadeth Lancelot to where Meliot
of Logres lay.   Lancelot sitteth him down
before him and asketh how it is with him?
'Meliot,' saith the damsel, 'This is Lancelot,
that bringeth you your healing.'   'Ha, Sir,
welcome may you be!'   'God grant you
health speedily,' saith Lancelot.   'Ha, for
God's sake,' saith Meliot, 'What doth Messire
Gawain?   Is he hearty?'   'I left him quite
hearty when I parted from him,' saith Lancelot,
'And so he knew that you had been wounded in
such sort, full sorry would he be thereof and
King Arthur likewise.'   'Sir,' saith he, 'The
knight that assieged them maimed me in this
fashion, but was himself maimed in such sort
that he is dead thereof.   But the wounds that
he dealt me are so cruel and so raging, that
they may not be healed save his sword toucheth
them and if they be not bound with some of
the winding-sheet wherein he was shrouded,
that he had displayed about him, all bloody.'
'By my faith,' saith the damsel, 'Behold them
here!'   'Ha, Sir,' saith he, 'Gramercy of
this great goodness!   In every way appeareth
it that you are good knight, for, but for the
goodness of your knighthood, the coffin wherein
the knight lieth had never opened so lightly,

Meliot nor would you never have had the sword nor
is healed the cloth, nor never till now hath knight entered
therein but either he were slain there, or departed thence wounded right grievously.' They
uncover his wounds, and Lancelot unbindeth
them, and the damsel toucheth him of the
sword and the winding-sheet, and they are
assuaged for him. And he saith that now at
last he knoweth well he need not fear to die
thereof. Lancelot is right joyful thereof in his
heart, for that he seeth he will be whole betimes;
and sore pity had it been of his death, for a
good knight was he, and wise and loyal.

XII

'Lancelot,' saith the lady, 'Long time have I
hated you on account of the knight that I loved,
whom you reft away from me and married to
another and not to me, and ofttimes have I put
myself to pains to grieve you of some ill deed
for that you did to me, for never was I so
sorrowful for aught that befell me. He loved
me of right great love, and I him again, and
never shall that love fail. But now is it far
further away from me than it was before, and
for this bounty that you have done, never
hereafter need you fear aught of my grievance.'
'Damsel,' saith Lancelot, 'Gramercy heartily.'
He was lodged in the castle the night richly
and worshipfully, and departed thence on the
morrow when he had taken leave of the damsel
and Meliot, and goeth back a great pace toward
the court of King Arthur, that was sore dismayed, for Madeglant was conquering his islands

and great part of his land. The more part of
the lands that he conquered had renounced the
New Law for fear of death and held the false
believe. And Messire Gawain and many other
knights were departed from King Arthur's
court for that the King trusted more in Briant
of the Isles than he did in them.

XIII

For many times had King Arthur sent
knights against Madeglant since Lancelot was
departed from the court, to the intent that they
should put to rebuke the enemies of his land,
but never saw he one come back from thence
nought discomfited. The King of Oriande
made much boast that he would fulfil for his
sister all that she had bidden him, for he
thought that King Arthur would yield himself
up betimes to him and yield all his land likewise.
The King greatly desired the return of Lancelot,
and said ofttimes that and he had been against
his enemies as nigh as the others he had sent
they would not have durst so to fly against him.
In the midst of the dismay wherein was King
Arthur, Lancelot returned to the court, whereof
was the King right joyous. Lancelot knew
that Messire Gawain and Messire Ywain were
not there, and that they held them aloof from
the court more willingly than they allowed
on account of Briant of the Isles, that King
Arthur believed in more than ever a one of
the others. He was minded to depart in like
sort, but the King would not let him, but said
to him rather, ' Lancelot, I pray and beseech

you, as him that I love much, that you set your
pains and your counsel on defending my land, for
great affiance have I in you.' 'Sir,' saith Lancelot,
'My aid and my force shall fail you never; take
heed that yours fail not me.' 'Of right ought
I not to fail you,' saith the King, 'Nor will I
never, for I should fail myself thereby.'

XIV

··The history saith that he gave Lancelot forty
knights in charge, and that he is come into an
island where King Madeglant was. Or ever
he knew of his coming, Lancelot had cut off
his retreat, for he cut his cables and beat his
anchors to pieces and broke up his ships. After
that, he struck among the people of Madeglant,
and slew as many of them as he would, he and
his knights. The King thought to withdraw
him back, both him and his fellowship, into
safety as he wont, but he found himself right ill
ill bested. Lancelot drove him toward the sea,
whither he fled, but only to find himself no less
decomfit there, and slew him in the midst of
his folk, and all his other knights were slain
and cast into the sea. This island was freed of
him by Lancelot, and from thence he went to
the other islands that Madeglant had conquered
and set again under the false Law, and there
did away the false Law from them that had
been set thereunder by fear of death, and
stablished the land in such sort as it had been
tofore. He roved so long from one island to
another that presently he came to Albanie where
he had succoured them at first.

XV

When they of the land saw him come, they well knew that the King of Oriande was dead and the islands made free, whereof made they great joy. The land was some deal emptied of the most puissant and the strongest, for they were dead along with their lord. Lancelot had brought with him some of the best knights and most puissant. He was come with a great navy into the land and began to destroy it. They of the land were misbelievers, for they believed in false idols and in false images. They saw that they might not defend the land, sith that their lord was dead. The more part let themselves be slain for that they would not renounce the evil Law, and they that were minded to turn to God were saved. The kingdom was right rich and right great that Lancelot conquered and attorned to the Law of Our Lord in such wise. He made break all the false images of copper and latten wherein they had believed tofore, and whereof false answers came to them of the voices of devils. Thereafter he caused be made crucifixes and images in the likeness of Our Lord, and in the likeness of His sweet Mother, the better to confirm them of the kingdoms in the Law.

XVI

The strongest and most valiant of the land assembled one day and said that it was high time a land so rich should no longer be without a King. They all agreed and came to Lance-

King Claudas lot and told him how they would fain that he should be King of the realm he had conquered, for in no land might he be better employed, and they would help him conquer other realms enow. Lancelot thanked them much, but told them that of this land nor of none other would he be King save by the approval of King Arthur only; for that all the conquest he had made was his, and by his commandment had he come thither, and had given him his own knights in charge that had helped him to reconquer the lands.

XVII

King Claudas had heard tell how Lancelot had slain the King of Oriande and that none of the islands might scarce be defended against him. He had no liking of him, neither of his good knighthood nor of his conquest, for well remembered he of the land that he had conquered from King Ban of Benoic that was Lancelot's father, and therefore was he sorry of the good knighthood whereof Lancelot was everywhere held of worth and renown, for that he was tenant of his father's land. King Claudas sent a privy message to Briant and bore him on hand that, and he might do so much as that King Arthur should forbid Lancelot his court, and that it were ill with him with the King, he would have much liking thereof and would help him betimes to take vengeance on his enemies, for, so Lancelot were forth of his court, and Messire Gawain, the rest would scarce abide long time; and thus should they have all their will of King Arthur's land. **Briant's** Briant sent word back to King Claudas that **treason** Messire Gawain and Messire Ywain began to hold them aloof from the court, and that as for most part of the other he need not trouble him a whit, for he might so deal as that in short time Lancelot should be well trounced, would they or nould they.

XVIII

Tidings are come to King Arthur's court that the King of Oriande is dead and his people destroyed, and that Lancelot hath conquered his kingdom and slain the King, and reconquered all the lands wherein he had set the false Law and the false believe by his force and by dread of him. And the more part say in the court that they of the realm of Oriande nor those of the other islands will not let Lancelot repair to court, and are doing their endeavour to make him King; and nought is there in the world, and he command them, they will not do, and that never was no folk so obedient to any as are they of all these lands to him. Briant of the Isles cometh one day privily to King Arthur, and saith: 'Sir,' saith he, 'Much ought I to love you, for that you have made me Seneschal of your land; whereby meseemeth you have great affiance in me, and my bounden duty is it to turn aside that which is evil from you and to set forward your good everywhere, and, did I not so, no whit loyal should I be towards you.

XIX

'Tidings are come to me of late that they of
the kingdom of Oriande and Albanie and of the
other islands that are your appanages have all
leagued together, and have sworn and given
surety that they will aid one another against
you, and they are going presently to make
Lancelot their King, and will come down upon
your land as speedily as they may wheresoever
he may dare lead them, and they have sworn
their oath that they will conquer your kingdom
just as you now hold it, and, so you be not
garnished against them betimes, you may have
thereof sore trouble to your own body as well
as the loss whereof I tell you.' 'By my head,'
saith the King, 'I believe not that Lancelot
durst think this, nor that he would have the
heart to do me evil.' 'By my head,' saith
Briant, 'Long time have I had misgivings both
of this and of him, but one ought not to tell
one's lord all that one knows, for that one
cannot be sure either that it be not leasing or
that folk wish to meddle in his affairs out of
envy. But nought is there in the world that I
will conceal from you henceforward for the love
that you bear me and for that you have affiance
in me, and so may you well have, for I have
abandoned my land for you that marched with
your own, whereby you may sorely straiten
your enemies, for well you know that in your
court is there no knight of greater power than
am I.'

XX

'By my head,' saith the King, 'I am fain to love you and hold you dear, nor shall you never be removed from my love nor from my service for nought that may be said of any, so manifestly have I seen your goodness and your loyalty. I will bid Lancelot by my letters and under my seal that he come to speak with me, for sore need have I thereof, and when he shall be here we will take account of this that you have told me, for this will I not, that he nor none other that may be my knight shall dare rise in arms against me, for such power ought lord of right to have over his knight, and to be feared and dreaded of him, for elsewise is he feeble, and lordship without power availeth nought.'

XXI

The King sent his letters by his messenger to Lancelot. The messenger sought him until he found him in the kingdom of Oriande, and delivered him the letters and the seal of the King. So soon as he knew that which the letters say, he took leave of them of the land, that were right sorrowful. He departed thence and came back to Cardoil, bringing with him all the knights that he had in charge, and told the King that he had reconquered for him all the islands, and that the King of Oriande was dead and that his land was attorned to the Law of Our Lord. The King bade Briant of the Isles that he should make forty knights come armed under their cloaks ready to take Lancelot

Lancelot
taken
prisoner

prisoner as soon as he should command them. The tidings come to Lancelot, there where he was in his hostel, that the King had made knights come all armed to the palace. Lancelot bethought him that some need had arisen and that he would arm himself likewise, so he made him be armed and came to the hall where the King was. 'Sir,' saith Briant, 'Lancelot thinketh him of something, for he hath armed himself at his hostel, and is come hither in such manner and at such time without your leave, and he may do something more yet. You ought well to ask him wherefore he wisheth to do you evil, and in what manner you have deserved it.' He biddeth him be called before him. 'Lancelot,' saith the King, 'Wherefore are you armed?' 'Sir, I was told that knights had come in hither armed, and I was feared lest some mishap had befallen you, for I would not that any evil should betide you.' 'You come hither for another thing,' saith the King, 'according to that I have been given to wit, and, had the hall been void of folk, you hoped to have slain me.' The King commandeth him be taken forthwith without gainsay of any. The knights that were armed did off their cloaks and leapt toward him on all sides, for they durst not disobey the King's commandment, and the more part were men of Briant of the Isles.

XXII

Lancelot seeth them coming towards him with their keen swords and saith, 'By my head, an evil guerdon do you return me of the services I have done for you.' The knights come to him all together swords drawn, and run upon him all at once. He goeth defending himself, as far as the wall of the hall, whereof he maketh a castle to his back, but before he cometh thither he hath slain or wounded seven. He began to defend himself right stoutly on all sides, but they give him great buffets of their swords, and no fair play is it of thirty or forty blows to one. Nor ought none believe that one single knight might deliver himself from so many men, seeing that they were eager to take him and to do him a hurt. Lancelot defended him the best he might, but the numbers were against him, and, anyway, or ever he let himself be taken he sold himself right dear, for of the forty knights he harmed at least a score, and of them was none that was not sore wounded and the most part killed; and he caught Briant of the Isles, that was helping to take him, so sore that he made his sword drink the blood of his body, in such sort that the wound was right wide. The knights laid hold on Lancelot on all sides, and the King commanded that none should harm him, but that they should bring him to his dungeon in the prison. Lancelot marvelled him much wherefore the King should do this, nor might he understand wherefore this hatred was come so lately. He is put in the prison so as the King hath commanded. All they of the court are sorry thereof, save Briant and his knights, but well may he yet aby it dear, so God bring Lancelot out of

A prison.   Some say, ' Now is the King's court
prophecy lost, sith that Messire Gawain and the other
knights have thus forsaken it, and Lancelot is
put in prison for doing well, ill trust may the
others have therein.'   They pray God yet
grant Briant of the Isles an evil guerdon, for
well know they that all this is of his procure-
ment.   And of an evil guerdon shall he not
fail so God protect Lancelot and bring him
forth of prison.

TITLE I

THEREUPON the story is silent of Aristot's
Lancelot, and cometh back to Perceval custom
that had not heard these tidings, and if he had
known them, right sorrowful would he have
been thereof. He is departed from his uncle's
castle that he hath reconquered, and was sore
grieved of the tidings that the damsel that was
wounded brought him of his sister that Aristot
had carried away by force to the house of a
vavasour. He was about to take her to wife
and cut off her head on the day of the New
Year, for such was his custom with all them
that he took. Perceval rideth one day, all
heavy in thought, and taketh his way as fast as
he may toward the hermitage of his uncle King
Hermit. He is come thither on an eventide,
and seeth three hermits issued forth of the
hermitage. He alighteth and goeth to meet
them so soon as he seeth them. 'Sir,' say the
hermits, 'Enter not in, for they are laying out
a body there.' 'Who is it?' saith Perceval.
'Sir,' say the hermits, 'It is the good King
Pelles that Aristot slew suddenly after mass on
account of one of his nephews, Perceval, whom
he loveth not, and a damsel is laying out the
body there within.' When Perceval heard the

news of his uncle that is dead, thereof was he right grieved at heart, and on the morrow was he at his uncle's burial.   When mass was sung, Perceval would have departed, as he that had great desire to take vengeance on him that had done him such shame.

II

Thereupon behold you the damsel that is his.   'Sir,' saith she, 'Full long time have I been seeking you.   Behold here the head of a knight that I carry hanging at the bow of my saddle, in this rich casket of ivory that you may see, and by none ought he to be avenged but by you alone.   Discharge me thereof, fair Sir, of your courtesy, for I have carried it too long a time, and this King Arthur knoweth well and Messire Gawain, for each hath seen me at court along with the head, but they could give me no tidings of you, and my castle may I not have again until such time as he be avenged.' 'Who, then, was the knight, damsel?' saith Perceval.   'Sir, he was son of your uncle Bruns Brandalis, and were he on live, would have been one of the best knights in the world.' 'And who slew him, damsel?' saith Perceval. 'Sir, the Knight of the Deep Forest that leadeth the lion, foully in treason there where he thought him safe.   For had he been armed in like manner as was the other, he would not have slain him.'   'Damsel,' saith Perceval, 'This grieveth me that he hath slain him, and it grieveth me likewise of mine uncle King Hermit, whom I would avenge more willingly

than all the men in the world, for he was slain
on my account.

III

'Most disloyal was this knight, and foully
was he fain to avenge him when he slew a holy
man, a hermit that never wished him ill on
account of me and of none other. Right glad
shall I be and I may find the knight, and so,
methinketh, will he be of me, for me he hateth
as much I do him, as I have been told, and
Lord God grant, howsoever he may take it,
that I may find him betimes. 'Sir,' saith the
damsel, 'So outrageous a knight is he that no
knight is there in the world so good but he
thinketh himself of more worth than he, and
sith that he hateth you with a will, and he
knew that you were here, you and another, or
you the third, he would come now at once, were
he in place and free.' 'Damsel,' saith Perceval,
'God give him mischief of his coming, come
whensoever he may!' 'Sir,' saith she, 'The
Deep Forest there, where the Red Knight
leadeth the lion, is towards the castle of Aristot,
and, or ever you come by adventure into the
forest, you may well hear some tidings of
him!'

BRANCH XXXII

Aristot and Dindrane HERE beginneth the last branch of the Graal in the name of the Father, and of the Son, and of the Holy Ghost.

TITLE I

The story saith that Perceval went his way through the forest. He saw pass before him two squires, and each carried a wild deer trussed behind him that had been taken by hounds. Perceval cometh to them a great pace and maketh them abide. 'Lords,' saith he, 'Whither will you carry this venison?' 'Sir,' say the squires, 'To the castle of Ariste, whereof Aristot is lord.' 'Is there great throng of knights at the castle?' saith Perceval. 'Sir,' say the squires, 'Not a single one is there, but within four days will be a thousand there, for Messire is about to marry, whereof is great preparation toward. He is going to take the daughter of the Widow Lady, whom he carried off by force before her castle of Camelot, and hath set her in the house of one of his vavasours until such time as he shall espouse her. But we are right sorrowful, for she is of most noble lineage and of great beauty and of the most worth in the world. So is it

great dole that he shall have her, for he will
cut her head off on the day of the New Year,
sith that such is his custom.' 'And one might
carry her off,' saith Perceval, 'would he not
do well therein?' 'Yea, Sir!' say the squires,
'Our Lord God would be well pleased thereof,
for such cruelty is the greatest that ever any
knight may have. Moreover, he is much
blamed of a good hermit that he hath slain, and
every day desireth he to meet the brother of the
damsel he is about to take, that is one of the
best knights in the world. And he saith that
he would slay him more gladly than ever another
knight on live.' 'And where is your lord?'
saith Perceval, 'Can you give me witting?'
'Yea, Sir,' say the squires, 'We parted from
him but now in this forest, where he held melly
with a knight that seemeth us to be right
worshipful and valiant, and saith that he hath
for name the Knight Hardy. And for that he
told Aristot that he was a knight of Perceval's
and of his fellowship, he ran upon him, and then
commanded us to come on, and said that he
should vanquish him incontinent. We could
still hear just now the blows of the swords
yonder where we were in the forest, and Aristot
is of so cruel conditions that no knight may
pass through this forest, but he is minded to
slay him.'

II

When Perceval heard these tidings, he departed from the squires, and so soon as they
were out of sight he goeth as great pace thither

as they had come thence. He had ridden half a league Welsh when he heard the buffets they were dealing one another on the helm with their swords, and right well pleased was he for that the Knight Hardy held so long time melly with Aristot in whom is there so much cruelty and felony. But Perceval knew not to what mischief the Knight Hardy had been wounded through the body of a spear, so that the blood rayed out on all sides; and Aristot had not remained whole, for he was wounded in two places. So soon as Perceval espied them, he smiteth his horse of his spurs, lance in rest, and smiteth Aristot right through the breast with such force that he maketh him lose his stirrups and lie down backwards over the hinder bow of the saddle. After that saith he: 'I am come to my sister's wedding, of right ought it not to be made without me.'

III

Aristot, that was full hardy, set himself again between the bows of the saddle in great wrath when he seeth Perceval, and cometh towards him like as if he were wood mad, sword in hand, and dealeth him such a buffet on the helm as that it is all dented in thereby. The Knight Hardy draweth back when he seeth Perceval, for he is wounded to the death through the body. He had held the stour so long time that he could abide no more. But or ever he departed, he had wounded Aristot in two places right grievously. Perceval felt the blow that was heavy, and that his helmet was dinted in.

He cometh back to Aristot and smiteth him **Perceval**
so passing strongly that he thrusteth the spear **slayeth**
right through his body and overthroweth him **Aristot**
and his horse all of a heap. Then he alighteth
over him and taketh off the coif of his habergeon
and unlaceth his ventail. 'What have you in
mind to do?' saith Aristot. 'I will cut off
your head,' saith Perceval, 'and present it to
my sister whom you have failed.' 'Do not
so!' saith Aristot, 'But let me live, and I will
forgo my hatred.' 'Your hatred might I well
abide henceforward, meseemeth,' saith Perceval,
'But one may not abide you any longer, for well
have you deserved this, and God willeth not to
bear with you.' He smiteth off his head incontinent and hangeth it at his saddle-bow, and
cometh to the Knight Hardy, and asketh him
how it is with him. 'Sir,' saith he, 'I am
very nigh my death, but I comfort me much of
this that I see you tofore I die.' Perceval is
remounted on his horse, then taketh his spear
and leaveth the body of the knight in the midst
of the launde, and so departeth forthwith and
leadeth the Knight Hardy to a hermitage that
was hard by there, and lifteth him down of his
horse as speedily as he may. After that, he
disarmed him and made him confess to the
hermit, and when he was shriven of his sins and
repentant, and his soul had departed, he made
him be enshrouded of the damsel that followed
him, and bestowed his arms and his horse on
the hermit for his soul, and the horse of Aristot
likewise.

IV

When mass had been sung for the knight that
was dead, and the body buried, Perceval departed. 'Sir,' saith the damsel that followed
him, 'Even now have you much to do. Of
this cruel knight and felonous you have avenged
this country. Now, God grant you find betimes the Red Knight that slew your uncle's
son. I doubt not but that you will conquer
him, but great misgiving have I of the lion, for
it is the cruellest beast that saw I ever, and he
so loveth his lord and his horse as never no beast
loved another so much, and he helpeth his lord
right hardily to defend him.'

V

Perceval goeth toward the great Deep Forest
without tarrying, and the damsel after. But, or
ever he came thither, he met a knight that was
wounded right sore, both he and his horse.
'Ha, Sir,' saith he to Perceval, 'Enter not into
this forest, whence I have scarce escaped with
much pains. For therein is a knight that had
much trouble of rescuing me from his lion; and
no less am I in dread to pass on forward, for
there is a knight that is called Aristot, that
without occasion runneth upon the knights that
pass through the forest.' 'Of him,' saith the
damsel, 'need you have no fear, for you may
see his head hanging at the knight's saddle-
bow.'

VI

'Certes,' saith the knight, 'Never yet was I
so glad of any tidings I have heard, and well
know I that he that slew him is not lacking of
great hardiment.' The knight departeth from
Perceval, but the lion had wounded his horse so
passing sore in the quarters that scarce could he
go. 'Sir Knight,' saith Perceval, 'Go to the
hermit in the Deep Forest, and say I bade him
give you the destrier I left with him, for well I
see that you have sore need thereof, and you
may repay him in some other manner, for rather
would he have something else than the horse.'
The knight giveth him much thanks of this that
he saith. He cometh to the hermit the best he
may, and telleth him according as he had been
charged, and the hermit biddeth him take which
destrier he will for the love of the knight that
had slain the evil-doer, that did so many evil
deeds in this forest. 'And I will lend you
them both twain if you will.' 'Sir,' saith the
knight, 'I ask but for one of them.' He
taketh Aristot's horse, that seemed him the
better, and straightway mounteth thereon, and
abandoneth his own, that might go no further.
He taketh leave of the hermit, and telleth him
he will right well repay him, but better had it
befallen him and he had not taken the horse,
for thereof was he slain without reason thereafter. A knight that was of the household of
Aristot overtook him at the corner of the forest,
and knew his lord's horse and had heard tell
that Aristot was dead, wherefore he went into

Perceval slayeth the lion the forest to bury him. He smote the knight through the body with his spear and so slew him, then took the horse and went away forthwith. But, had Perceval known thereof, he would have been little glad, for that he asked the knight to go for the horse, but he did it only for the best, and for that he rode in great misease.

VII

Perceval goeth toward the Deep Forest, that is full broad and long and evil seeming, and when he was entered in, he had scarce ridden a space when he espied the lion that lay in the midst of a launde under a tree and was waiting for his master, that was gone afar into the forest, and the lion well knew that just there was the way whereby knights had to pass, and therefore had abided there. The damsel draweth her back for fear, and Perceval goeth toward the lion that had espied him already, and came toward him, eyes on fire and jaws yawning wide. Perceval aimeth his spear and thinketh to smite him in his open mouth, but the lion swerved aside and he caught him in the fore-leg and so dealt him a great wound, but the lion seizeth the horse with his claws on the croup, and rendeth the skin and the flesh above the tail. The horse, that feeleth himself wounded, catcheth him with his two hinder feet or ever he could get away, so passing strongly that he breaketh the master-teeth in his jaw. The lion gave out a roar so loud that all the forest resounded thereof. The Red Knight heareth his lion roar, and so cometh thither a **and** great gallop, but, or ever he was come thither, **the Red** Perceval had slain the lion. When the knight **Knight** saw his lion dead, right sorry was he thereof. 'By my head,' saith he to Perceval, 'When you slew my lion you did it as a traitor!' 'And you,' saith Perceval, 'adjudged your own death when you slew my uncle's son, whose head this damsel beareth.' Perceval cometh against him without more words, and the knight in like manner with a great rushing, and breaketh his spear upon his shield. Perceval smiteth him with such force that he thrusteth his spear right through his body and beareth him to the ground dead beside his horse. Perceval alighteth of his own when he hath slain the knight, and then mounteth him on the Red Knight's horse for that his own might carry him no longer.

VIII

'Sir,' saith the damsel, 'My castle is in the midst of this forest, that the Red Knight reft away from me long ago. I pray you now come with me thither that I may be assured thereof in such sort as that I may have it again wholly.' 'Damsel,' saith Perceval, 'This have I no right to deny you.' They ride amidst the forest so long as that they come to the castle where the damsel ought to be. It stood in the fairest place of all the forest, and was enclosed of high walls battlemented, and within were fair-windowed halls. The tidings were come to the castle that their lord was dead.

Dindrane Perceval and the damsel entered in.   He made
lamenteth the damsel be assured of them that were therein,
and made them yield up her castle that they
well knew was hers of right inheritance.   The
damsel made the head be buried that she had
carried so long, and bade that every day should
mass be done within for the soul of him.   When
Perceval had sojourned therein as long as pleased
him, he departed thence.   The damsel thanked
him much of the bounty he had done her as concerning the castle that she had again by him, for
never again should it be reconquered of another,
as well she knew.

IX

Josephus telleth us in the scripture he recordeth
for us, whereof this history was drawn out of
Latin into Romance, that none need be in doubt
that these adventures befell at that time in Great
Britain and in all the other kingdoms, and plenty
enow more befell than I record, but these were
the most certain.   The history saith that
Perceval is come into a hold, there where his
sister was in the house of a vavasour that was
a right worshipful man.   Each day the damsel
made great dole of the knight that was to take
her, for the day was already drawing somewhat
nigh, and she knew not that he was dead.   Full
often lamented she the Widow Lady her mother,
that in like sort made great dole for her daughter.
The vavasour comforted the damsel right sweetly
and longed for her brother Perceval, but little
thought he that he was so near him.   And
Perceval is come to the hold all armed, and

alighteth at the mounting-stage before the hall. **Perceval**
The vavasour cometh to meet him, and marvelleth **com-**
much who he is, for the more part believed that **forteth**
he was one of Aristot's knights. 'Sir,' saith **her**
the vavasour, 'Welcome may you be!' 'Good
adventure may you have, Sir!' saith Perceval.
He holdeth Aristot's head in his hand by the
hair, whereof the vavasour marvelled much that
he should carry a knight's head in such-wise.
Perceval cometh to the master-chamber of the
hall, where his sister was, that bewailed her
right sore.

x

'Damsel,' saith he to his sister, 'Weep not,
for your wedding hath failed. You may know
it well by this token!' He throweth the head
of Aristot before her on the ground, then saith
to her : 'Behold here the head of him that was
to take you!' The damsel heareth Perceval her
brother that was armed, and thereby she knoweth
him again. She leapeth up and maketh him the
greatest joy that ever damsel made to knight.
She knoweth not what to do. So joyful is she,
that all have pity on her that see her of her
weeping for the joy that she maketh of her
brother. The story saith that they sojourned
therewithin and that the vavasour showed them
much honour. The damsel made cast the
knight's head into a river that ran round about
the hold. The vavasour was right glad of his
death for the great felony that he had in him,
and for that needs must the damsel die in less
than a year and she had espoused him.

XI

When Perceval had been therein as long as
it pleased him, he thanked the vavasour much of
the honour he had done him and his sister, and
departed, he and his sister along with him on
the mule whereon she had been brought thither.
Perceval rode so long on his journeys that he is
come to Camelot and findeth his mother in
great dole for her daughter that should be
Queen, for she thought surely that never should
she see her more. Full sorrowful was she
moreover of her brother, the King Hermit that
had been killed in such-wise. Perceval cometh
to the chamber where his mother was lying and
might not stint of making dole. He taketh his
sister by the hand and cometh before her. So
soon as she knoweth him she beginneth to weep
for joy, and kisseth them one after the other.
'Fair son,' saith she, 'Blessèd be the hour that
you were born, for by you all my great joy
cometh back to me! Now well may I depart,
for I have lived long enow.' 'Lady,' saith he,
'Your life ought to be an offence to none, for to
none hath it ever done ill, but, please God, you
shall not end in this place, but rather you shall
end in the castle that was your cousin's german,
King Fisherman, there where is the most Holy
Graal and the sacred hallows are.' 'Fair son,'
saith she, 'You say well, and there would I
fain be.' 'Lady,' saith he, 'God will provide
counsel and means whereby you shall be there;
and my sister, and she be minded to marry, will
we set in good place, where she may live worship-

fully.' 'Certes, fair brother,' saith she, 'None return to
shall I never marry, save God alone.' 'Fair Camelot
son,' saith the Widow Lady, 'The Damsel of
the Car goeth to seek you, and I shall end not
until such time as she hath found you.' 'Lady,'
saith he, 'In some place will she have tidings of
me and I of her.' 'Fair son,' saith the Lady,
'The damsel is here within that the felonous
knight wounded through the arm, that carried
off your sister, but she is healed.' 'Lady,' saith
he, 'I am well avenged.' He telleth her all the
adventures until the time when he reconquered
the castle that was his uncle's. He sojourned
long time with his mother in the castle, and saw
that the land was all assured and peaceable.
He departed thence and took his leave, for
he had not yet achieved all that he had to do.
His mother remained long time, and his sister,
at Camelot, and led a good life and a holy. The
lady made make a chapel right rich about the
sepulchre that lay between the forest and
Camelot, and had it adorned of rich vestments,
and stablished a chaplain that should sing mass
there every day. Sithence then hath the place
been so builded up as that there is an abbey
there and folk of religion, and many bear witness
that there it is still, right fair. Perceval was
departed from Camelot and entered into the
great forest, and so rode of a long while until
he had left his mother's castle far behind, and
came toward evening to the hold of a knight
that was at the head of the forest. He
harboured him therein, and the knight showed
him much honour and made him be unarmed,

and brought him a robe to do on. Perceval seeth that the knight is a right simple man, and that he sigheth from time to time.

XII

'Sir,' saith he, 'Meseemeth you are not over joyous.' 'Certes, Sir,' saith the knight, 'I have no right to be, for a certain man slew mine own brother towards the Deep Forest not long since, and no right have I to be glad, for a worshipful man was he and a loyal.' 'Fair Sir,' saith Perceval, 'Know you who slew him?' 'Fair Sir, it was one of Aristot's knights, for that he was sitting upon a horse that had been Aristot's, and whereon another knight had slain him, and a hermit had lent him to my brother for that the Red Knight's lion had maimed his own.' Perceval was little glad of these tidings, for that he had sent him that had been slain on account of the horse. 'Sir,' saith Perceval, 'Your brother had not deserved his death, methinketh, for it was not he that slew the knight.' 'No, Sir, I know it all of a truth, but another, that slew the Red Knight of the Deep Forest.' Perceval was silent thereupon. He lay the night at the hostel and was harboured right well, and on the morrow departed when he had taken leave. He wandered until he came to a hermitage there where he heard mass. After the service, the hermit came to him and said: 'Sir,' saith he, 'In this forest are knights all armed that are keeping watch for the knight that slew Aristot and the Red Knight and his lion as well.

Wherefore they meet no knight in this forest **Perceval**
but they are minded to slay him for the knight **slayeth**
that slew these twain.' 'Sir,' saith Perceval, **two**
'God keep me from meeting such folk as would **knights**
do me evil.'

XIII

With that he departed from the hermitage
and took leave of the hermit, and rideth until
that he is come into the forest and espieth the
knight that sitteth on Aristot's horse for that he
hath slain the other knight. A second knight
was with him. They abide when they see
Perceval. 'By my head,' saith one of them,
'This same shield bare he that slew Aristot, as
it was told us, and, like enough, it may be he.'
They come toward him, full career. Perceval
seeth them coming, and forgetteth not his spurs,
but rather cometh against them the speediest he
may. The two knights smote him upon the
shield and brake their spears. Perceval overtaketh him that sitteth on Aristot's horse and
thrusteth an ell's length of his spear through his
body and so overthroweth him dead.

XIV

After that, he cometh to the other knight,
that fain would have fled, and smiteth off the
shoulder close to his side, and he fell dead by
the side of the other. He taketh both twain of
their destriers, and knotteth the reins together
and driveth them before him as far as the house
of the hermit, that had issued forth of his
hermitage. He delivered to him the horse of

Aristot, and the other of the knight that he had
sent thither. 'Sir,' saith Perceval, 'Well I
know that and you shall see any knight that
hath need of it and shall ask you, you will lend
him one of these horses, for great courtesy is it
to aid a worshipful man when one seeth him in
misfortune.' 'Sir,' saith the hermit, 'But now
since, were here three knights. So soon as
they knew that the two were dead whose horses
you have delivered to me, they departed, fleeing
the speediest they might. I praised them much
of their going, and told them they did well not
to die on such occasion, for that the souls of
knights that die under arms are nigher to Hell
than Paradise.'

XV

Perceval, that never was without sore toil
and travail so long as he lived, departed from
the hermitage and went with great diligence
right through the midst of the forest, and met
a knight that came a great gallop over against
him. He knew Perceval by the shield that he
bare. 'Sir,' saith he, 'I come from the Castle
of the Black Hermit, there where you will find
the Damsel of the Car as soon as you arrive,
wherefore she sendeth you word by me that you
speed your way and go to her to ask for the chess-
board that was taken away from before Messire
Gawain, or otherwise never again will you enter
into the castle you have won. Sir,' saith he,
'Haste, moreover, on account of a thing most
pitiful that I heard in this forest. I heard how
a knight was leading a damsel against her will,

beating her with a great scourge. I passed **A**
by the launde on the one side and he on the **churlish**
other, so that I espied him through the under- **knight**
wood that was between us; but it seemed me
that the damsel was bemoaning her for the son
of the Widow Lady that had given her back
her castle, and the knight said that for love
of him he would put her into the Serpent's pit.
An old knight and a priest went after the knight
to pray him have mercy on the damsel, but
so cruel is he, that so far from doing so, he
rather waxed sore wroth for that they prayed it
of him, and made cheer and semblant as though
he would have slain them.' The knight departeth from Perceval and taketh leave, and
Perceval goeth along the way that the knight
had come, thinking that he would go after the
damsel, for he supposeth certainly that it is she
to whom he gave back her castle, and would
fain know what knight it is that entreateth her
in such fashion. He hath ridden until he is
come into the deepest of the forest and the
thickest. He bideth awhile and listeneth and
heareth the voice of the damsel, that was in
a great valley where the Serpent's pit was,
wherein the knight was minded to set her.
She cried right loud for mercy, and wept, and
the knight gave her great strokes of the scourge
to make her be still. Perceval had no will
to tarry longer, but rather cometh thither as
fast as he may.

XVI

So soon as the damsel seeth Perceval, she
knoweth him again. She claspeth her two

hands together and saith, 'Ha, Sir, for God's sake have mercy! Already have you given me back the castle whereof this knight would reave me.' The horse whereon Perceval sat, the knight knew him. 'Sir,' saith he, 'This horse was the horse of Messire the Red Knight of the Deep Forest! Now at last know I that it was you that slew him!' 'It may well be,' saith Perceval, 'And if that I slew him, good right had I to do so, for he had cut off the head of a son of mine uncle, the which head this damsel carried of a long time.' 'By my head,' saith the knight, 'Sith that you slew him, you are my mortal enemy!' So he draweth off in the midst of the launde and Perceval likewise, and then they come together as fast as their horses may carry them, and either giveth other great buffets in the midst of their breast with their spears the most they may. Perceval smiteth the knight so passing hard that he overthroweth him to the ground right over the croup of his horse, and in the fall that he made, he to-brake him the master-bone of his leg so that he might not move. And Perceval alighteth to the ground and cometh where the knight lay. And he crieth him mercy that he slay him not. And Perceval telleth him he need not fear death, nor that he is minded to slay him in such plight as he is, but that like as he was fain to make the damsel do he will make him do. He maketh alight the other old knight and the priest, then maketh the knight be carried to the Pit of the Serpent and the worms, whereof was great store. The pit was dark and deep.

When that the knight was therein he might **An evil**
not live long for the worms that were there. **believe**
The damsel thanked Perceval much of this
goodness and of the other that he had done
her. She departeth and returneth again to
her castle, and was assured therein on all sides,
nor never thereafter had she dread of no knight,
for the cruel justice that Perceval had done on
this one.

XVII

The son of the Widow Lady of his good
knighthood knoweth not how to live without
travail. He well knoweth that when he hath
been at the Black Hermit's castle, he will in
some measure have achieved his task. But
many another thing behoveth him to do tofore,
and little toil he thinketh it, whereof shall God
be well pleased. He hath ridden so far one
day and another, that he came into a land where
he met knights stout and strong there where
God was neither believed in nor loved, but
where rather they adored false images and false
Lord-Gods and devils that made themselves
manifest. He met a knight at the entrance of
a forest. 'Ha, Sir!' saith he to Perceval,
'Return you back! No need is there for you
to go further, for the folk of this island are not
well-believers in God. I may not pass through
the land but by truce only. The Queen of
this land was sister of the King of Oriande,
that Lancelot killed in the battle and all his
folk, and seized his land, wherein all the folk
were misbelievers. Now throughout all the

Queen land they believe in the Saviour of the World.
Jandree Thereof is she passing sorrowful, and hateth
all them that believe in the New Law, insomuch
as that she would not look upon any that
believed, and prayed to her gods that never
might she see none until such time as the New
Law should be overthrown; and God, that
hath power to do this, blinded her forthwith.
Now she supposeth that the false gods wherein
she believeth have done this, and saith that
when the New Law shall fall, she will have
her sight again by the renewal of these gods,
and by their virtue, nor, until this hour, hath
she no desire to see. And I tell you this,'
saith the knight, 'because I would not that you
should go thither as yet, for that I misdoubt of
your being troubled thereby.' 'Sir, gramercy,'
saith Perceval, 'But no knighthood is there so
fair as that which is undertaken to set forward
the Law of God, and for Him ought one to
make better endeavour than for all other. In
like manner as He put His body in pain and
travail for us, so ought each to put his own for
Him.' He departeth from the knight, and
was right joyous of this that he heard him say
that Lancelot had won a kingdom wherein he
had done away the false Law. But and he
knew the tidings that the King had put him
in prison, he would not have been glad at all,
for Lancelot was of his lineage and was therefore good knight, and for this he loved him
right well.

XVIII

Perceval rideth until nightfall, and findeth a great castle fortified with a great drawbridge, and there were tall ancient towers within. He espied at the door a squire that had the weight of a chain on his neck, and at the other end the chain was fixed to a great bulk of iron. The chain was as long as the length of the bridge. Then cometh he over against Perceval when he seeth him coming. 'Sir,' saith he, 'Meseemeth you believe in God?' 'Fair friend, so do I, the best I may.' 'Sir, for God's sake, enter not this castle!' 'Wherefore, fair friend?' saith Perceval. 'Sir,' saith he, 'I will tell you. I am Christian, even as are you, and I am thrall within there and guard this gate, as you see. But it is the most cruel castle that I know, and it is called the Raving Castle. There be three knights within there, full young and comely, but so soon as they see a knight of the New Law, forthwith are they out of their senses, and all raving mad, so that nought may endure between them. Moreover, there is within one of the fairest damsels that saw I ever. She guardeth the knights so soon as they begin to rave, and so much they dread her that they durst not disobey her commandment in aught that she willeth, for many folk would they evilly entreat were it not for her. And for that I am their thrall they put up with me, and I have no fear of them, but many is the Christian knight that hath come in hither that never hath issued hence.' 'Fair sweet friend,'

Three saith Perceval, 'I will enter in thither and I
brothers may, for I should not know this day how to gc
elsewhither, and true it is that greater power
hath God than the devil.' He entereth into
the castle and alighteth in the midst of the
courtyard.

XIX

The damsel was at the windows of the hall,
that was of passing great beauty. She cometh
down as soon as she may, and seeth Perceval
come in and the cross on his shield, and
knoweth well thereby that he is Christian.
'Ha, Sir, for God's sake,' saith she, 'Come
not up above, for there be three of the comeliest
knights that ever were seen that are playing at
tables and at dice in a chamber, and they are
brothers-german. They will all go out of their
senses so soon as they shall see you!'

XX

'Damsel,' saith Perceval, 'Please God, so
shall they not, and such a miracle is good to
see, for it is only right that all they who will
not believe in God should be raving mad when
they see the things that come of Him.' Perceval
goeth up into the hall, all armed, for all that
the damsel saith. She followeth him as fast as
she may. The three knights espied Perceval
all armed and the cross on his shield, and
forthwith leapt up and were beside themselves.
They rolled their eyes and tore themselves and
roared like devils. There were axes and
swords in the hall that they go to lay hold
on, and they are fain to leap upon Perceval,

but no power have they to do so, for such was **slay each other** the will of God. When they saw that they might not come a-nigh him, they ran either on other and so slew themselves between them, nor would they stint their fighting together for the damsel. Perceval beheld the miracle of these folks that were thus killed, and the damsel that made right great dole thereof. 'Ha, damsel,' saith he, 'Weep not, but repent you of this false believe, for they that are unwilling to believe in God shall die like mad folks and devils!' Perceval made the squires that were there within bear the bodies out of the hall, and made them be cast into a running water, and straightway slew all the other, for that they were not minded to believe. The castle was all emptied of the misbelieving folk save only the damsel and those that waited upon her, and the Christian thrall that guarded the gate. Perceval set him forth of the chain, then led him up into the hall and made him disarm him. He found sundry right rich robes. The damsel, that was of right great beauty, looked at him and saw that he was a full comely knight, and well pleased she was with him. She honoured him in right great sort, but she might not forget the three knights that were her brothers, and made sore dole for them.

XXI

'Damsel,' saith Perceval, 'Nought availeth it to make this dole, but take comfort on some other manner.' Perceval looked at the hall from one end to the other and saw that it was

A right rich, and the damsel, in whom was full
damsel great beauty, stinted of making dole to look at
loveth Perceval.   She seeth that he is comely knight
and gentle and tall and well furnished of good
conditions, wherefore he pleaseth her much, and
forthwith beginneth she to love him, and saith to
herself that, so he would leave his God for the
god in whom she believed, right glad would
she be thereof, and would make him lord of her
castle, for it seemed her that better might she
not bestow it, and, sith that her brothers are
dead, there may be no bringing of them back,
and therefore better would it be to forget her
dole.   But little knew she Perceval's thought,
for had she known that which he thinketh, she
would have imagined not this ; for, and had she
been Christian he might not have been drawn to
love her in such sort as she thinketh, sith that
Josephus telleth us that never did he lose his
virginity for woman, but rather died virgin and
chaste and clean of his body.   In this mind
was she still, nor never might she refrain her
heart from him.   Thinketh she rather that, and
he knew she was minded to love him, right
joyous would he be thereof, for that she is of
so passing beauty.   Perceval asketh the damsel
what she hath in her thought ? 'Sir,' saith she,
'Nought think I but only good and you will.'
'Damsel,' saith Perceval, 'Never, please God,
shall there be hindrance of me but that you
renounce this evil Law and believe in the good.'
'Sir,' saith she, 'Do you renounce yours for
love of me, and I will do your commandment
and your will.'

XXII

'Damsel,' saith Perceval, 'Nought availeth to tell me this. Were you man like as you are woman, your end would have come with the others. But, please God, your tribulation shall lend itself to good.' 'Sir,' saith she, 'So you are willing to promise me that you will love me like as knight ought to love damsel, I am well inclined to believe in your God.' 'Damsel, I promise you as I am a Christian that so you are willing to receive baptism, I will love you as he that firmly believeth in God ought to love damsel.' 'Sir,' saith she, 'I ask no more of you.' She biddeth send for a holy man, a hermit that was in the forest appurtenant, and right gladly came he when he heard the tidings. They held her up and baptized her, both her and her damsels with her. Perceval held her at the font. Josephus witnesseth us in this history that she had for name Celestre. And great joy made she of her baptism, and her affections turned she to good. The hermit remained there with her, and taught her to understand the firm believe, and did the service of Our Lord. The damsel was of right good life and right holy, and ended thereafter in many good works.

XXIII

Perceval departed from the castle, and gave thanks to Our Lord and praise, that He hath allowed him to conquer a castle so cruel and to attorn it to the Law. He went his way a great pace, all armed, until he came into a country

Queen wherein was great grief being made, and the
Jandree more part said that he was come that should
destroy their Law, for that already had he won
their strongest castle. He is come towards an
ancient castle that was at the head of a forest.
He looketh and seeth at the entrance of the
gateway a full great throng of folk. He seeth
a squire come forth thence, and asketh him to
whom belongeth the castle. 'Sir,' saith he,
'It is Queen Jandree's, that hath made her be
brought before her gate with the folk you see
yonder, for she hath heard tell how the knights
of the Raving Castle are dead, and another
knight that hath conquered the castle hath made
the damsel be baptized, wherefore much she
marvelleth how this may be. She is in much
dread of losing her land, for her brother
Madeglant of Oriande is dead, so that she may
no longer look to none for succour, and she
hath been told how the knight that conquered
the Raving Castle is the Best Knight of the
World, and that none may endure against him.
For this doubtance and fear of him she is
minded to go to one of her own castles that is
somewhat stronger.' Perceval departeth from
the squire and rideth until they that were at the
entrance of the gateway espied him. They
saw the Red Cross that he bare on his shield,
and said to the Queen, 'Lady, a Christian
knight is coming into this castle.' 'Take heed,'
saith she, 'that it be not he that is about to
overthrow our Law!' Perceval cometh thither
and alighteth, and cometh before the Queen all
armed. The Queen asketh what he seeketh.

XXIV

'Lady,' saith he, 'Nought seek I save good only to yourself so you hinder it not.' 'You come,' saith she, 'from the Raving Castle, there where three brothers are slain, whereof is great loss.' 'Lady,' saith he, 'At that castle was I, and now fain would I that your own were at the will of Jesus Christ, in like manner as is that.' 'By my head,' saith she, 'And your Lord hath so great power as is said, so will it be.' 'Lady, His virtue and His puissance are far greater than they say.' 'That would I fain know,' saith she, 'presently, and I am fain to pray you that you depart not from me until that it hath been proven.' Perceval granteth it gladly. She returned into her castle and Perceval with her. When he was alighted he went up into the hall. They that were within marvelled them much that she should thus give consent, for never, sithence that she had been blind, might she allow no knight of the New Law to be so nigh her, and made slay all them that came into her power, nor might she never see clear so long as she had one of them before her. Now is her disposition altered in such sort as that she would fain she might see clear him that hath come in, for she hath been told that he is the comeliest knight of the world and well seemeth to be as good as they witness of him.

XXV

Perceval remained there gladly for that he saw the lady's cruelty was somewhat slackened,

and it seemed him that it would be great joy
and she were willing to turn to God, and they
that are within there, for well he knoweth that
so she should hold to the New Law, all they of
the land would be of the same mind. When
Perceval had lain the night at the castle, the
Lady on the morrow sent for all the more
powerful of her land, and came forth of her
chamber into the hall where Perceval was,
seeing as clear as ever she had seen aforetime.
'Lords,' saith she, 'Hearken ye all, for now
will I tell you the truth like as it hath befallen
me.   I was lying in my bed last night, and well
know ye that I saw not a whit, and made my
orisons to our gods that they would restore me
my sight.   It seemed me they made answer
that they had no power so to do, but that I
should make be slain the knight that was arrived
here, and that and I did not, sore wroth would
they be with me.   And when I had heard their
voices say that nought might they avail me as
for that I had prayed of them, I remembered
me of the Lord in whom they that hold the
New Law believe.   I prayed Him right sweetly
that, and so it were that He had such virtue
and such puissance as many said, He would
make me see clear, so as that I might believe
in Him.   At that hour I fell on sleep, and
meseemed that I saw one of the fairest Ladies
in the world, and she was delivered of a Child
therewithin, and He had about Him a great
brightness of light like it were the sun shone at
right noonday.

XXVI

'When the Child was born, so passing fair was He and so passing gentle and of so sweet semblant that the looks of Him pleased me well; and meseemed that at His deliverance there was a company of folk the fairest that were seen ever, and they were like as it had been birds and made full great joy. And methought that an ancient man that was with Her, told me that My Lady had lost no whit of her maidenhood for the Child. Well pleased was I the while this thing lasted me. It seemed me that I saw it like as I do you. Thereafter, methought I saw a Man bound to a stake, in whom was great sweetness and humility, and an evil folk beat Him with scourges and rods right cruelly, so that the blood ran down thereof. They would have no mercy on Him. Of this might I not hold myself but that I wept for pity of Him. Therewithal I awoke and marvelled much whence it should come and what it might be. But in anyway it pleased me much that I had seen it. It seemed me after this, that I saw the same Man that had been bound to the stake set upon a cross, and nailed thereon right grievously and smitten in the side with a spear, whereof had I such great pity that needs must I weep of the sore pain that I saw Him suffer. I saw the Lady at the feet of the cross, and knew her again that I had seen delivered of the Child, but none might set in writing the great dole that she made. On the other side of the cross was a man that

The seemed not joyful, but he recomforted the Lady
Graal the fairest he might. And another folk were
there that collected His blood in a most holy
Vessel that one of them held for it.

XXVII

'Afterward, methought I saw Him taken
down of hanging on the cross, and set in a
sepulchre of stone. Thereof had I great pity,
for, so long as meseemed I saw Him thus,
never might I withhold me from weeping.
And so soon as the pity came into my heart,
and the tears into my eyes, I had my sight even
as you see. In such a Lord as this ought one
to believe, for He suffered death when He
might lightly have avoided it had He so willed,
but He did it to save His people. In this Lord
I will that ye all believe, and so renounce our
false gods, for they be devils and therefore may
not aid us nor avail us. And he that will not
believe, him will I make be slain or die a
shameful death.' The Lady made her be held
up and baptized, and all them that would not
do the same she made be destroyed and
banished. This history telleth us that her
name was Salubre. She was good lady and
well believed in God, and so holy life led
she thereafter that in a hermitage she died.
Perceval departed from the castle right joyous
in his heart of the Lady and her people that
believed in the New Law.

BRANCH XXXIII

TITLE I

AFTERWARD, this title telleth us that Meliot of Meliot of Logres was departed from Logres Castle Perilous sound and whole, by virtue of the sword that Lancelot had brought him, and of the cloth that he took in the Chapel Perilous. But sore sorrowful was he of the tidings he had heard that Messire Gawain was in prison and he knew not where, but he had been borne on hand that two knights that were kinsmen of them of the Raving Castle that had slain one another, had shut him in prison on account of Perceval that had won the castle. Now, saith Meliot of Logres, never shall he have ease again until he knoweth where Messire Gawain is. He rideth amidst a forest, and prayeth God grant him betimes to hear witting of Messire Gawain. The forest was strange and gloomy. He rode until nightfall but might not find neither hold nor hermitage. He looketh right amidst the forest before him and seeth a damsel sitting that bemoaneth herself full sore. The moon was dark and the place right foul of seeming and the forest gloomy of shadow. 'Ha, damsel, and what do you here at this hour?' 'Sir,' saith she, 'I may not amend it, the more is my sorrow. For the place is more perilous than you think. Look,' saith she,

Two 'up above, and you will see the occasion
knights wherefore I am here.' Meliot looketh and
hanging seeth two knights all armed hanging up above
the damsel's head. Thereof much marvelleth
he. 'Ha, damsel,' saith he, 'Who slew these
knights so foully?' 'Sir,' saith she, 'The
Knight of the Galley that singeth in the sea.'
'And wherefore hath he hanged them in such
wise?' 'For this,' saith she, 'that they
believed in God and His sweet Mother. And
so behoveth me to watch them here for forty
days, that none take them down of hanging,
for and they were taken hence he would lose
his castle, he saith, and would cut off my head.'
'By my head,' saith Meliot, 'Such watch is
foul shame to damsel, and no longer shall you
remain here.' 'Ha, Sir,' saith the damsel,
'Then shall I be a dead woman, for he is of
so great cruelty that none scarce might protect
me against him.'

II

'Damsel,' saith Meliot, 'Foul shame would
it be and I left here these knights in such wise
for the reproach of other knights.' Meliot
made them graves with his sword, and so
buried them the best he might. 'Sir,' saith
the damsel, 'And you take not thought to
protect me, the knight will slay me. To-
morrow, when he findeth not the knights, he
will search all the forest to look for me.'
Meliot and the damsel together go their way
through the forest until they come to a chapel
where was wont to be a hermit that the Knight

of the Galley had destroyed.   He helpeth
down the damsel of his horse, and afterward
they entered into the chapel, where was a great
brightness of light, and a damsel was there
that kept watch over a dead knight.   Meliot
marvelleth him much.   ' Damsel,' saith Meliot,
' When was this knight killed ? '   ' Sir, yesterday the Knight of the Galley slew him on the
sea-shore, wherefore behoveth me thus keep
watch, and in the morning will he come hither
or ever he go to the castle where Messire
Gawain hath to-morrow to fight with a lion,
all unarmed, and my Lady, that is mistress
both of me and of this damsel you have brought
hither, will likewise be brought to-morrow to
the place where the lion is to slay Messire
Gawain, and she in like sort will be afterward
delivered to the lion and she renounce not the
New Law wherein the knight that came from
Raving Castle, whereof she is lady, hath made
her believe ; and we ourselves shall be in like
manner devoured along with her.   But this
damsel would still have taken respite of my
death and she had still kept guard over the
knights that were so foully hanged above her.
Natheless, sith that you have taken them down
from where they were hanging, you have done a
right good deed, whatsoever betide, for the Lord
of the Red Tower will give his castle to the
knight for this.'   Meliot is right joyous of the
tidings that he hath heard of Messire Gawain
that he is still on live, for well knoweth he, sith
that the Knight of the Galley will come by the
chapel there, that he will come thither or ever

Messire Gawain doth battle with the lion.
'Sir,' saith the damsel of the chapel, 'For
God's sake, take this damsel to a place of
safety, for the knight will be so wood mad of
wrath and despite so soon as he cometh hither,
that he will be fain to smite off her head
forthwith, and of yourself also have I great
fear.'

III

'Damsel,' saith Meliot, 'The knight is but a
man like as am I.' 'Yea, Sir, but stronger is
he and more cruel than seem you to be.' Meliot
was in the chapel the night until the morrow,
and heard the knight coming like a tempest, and
he brought with him the lady of the castle and
reviled her from time to time, and Meliot seeth
him come, and a dwarf that followeth after him
a great pace. He crieth out to him: 'Sir,
behold there the disloyal knight through whom
you have lost your castle. Now haste! Avenge
yourself of him! After that will we go to the
death of Messire Gawain?' Meliot, so soon as
he espieth him, mounteth and maketh his arms
ready. 'Is it you,' saith the Knight of the
Galley, 'that hath trespassed on my demesne
and taken down my knights?' 'By my head,
yours were they not! Rather were they the
knights of God, and foul outrage have you done
herein when you slew them so shamefully.'
He goeth toward the knight without more
words, and smiteth him so passing strong amidst
the breast that he pierceth the habergeon and
thrusteth all the iron of his spear into his body

and afterward draweth it back to him with a **Meliot** great wrench. And the knight smiteth him so **slayeth** hard on his shield that he maketh an ell's length **him** pass beyond, for right wroth was he that he was wounded. The dwarf crieth to him, 'Away, then! The knight endureth against you that have slain so many of them!' The Knight of the Galley waxeth wood wrath. He taketh his career, and cometh as fast as his horse may carry him, and smiteth Meliot so strongly that he breaketh his spear in such sort that he maketh both him and his horse stagger. But Meliot catcheth him better, for he thrusteth the spear right through his body and hurleth against him at the by-passing with such stoutness and force that he maketh him fall dead to the ground from his horse. The dwarf thought to escape, but Meliot smote off his head, whereof the damsels gave him great thanks, for many a mischief had he wrought them.

IV

Meliot buried the knight that he found in the chapel dead, then told the damsels that he might abide no longer, but would go succour Messire Gawain and he might. The damsels were horsed to their will, for one had the horse of the knight that was slain and the other the horse of the dwarf. The other damsel was come upon a mule, and they said that they would go back, for the country was made all safe by the death of the knight. They thanked Meliot much, for they say truly that he hath rescued them from death. Meliot departeth from the

Gawain
in sore
peril
damsels and goeth right amidst the forest as he that would most fain hear tidings of Messire Gawain. When he had ridden of a long space, he met a knight that was coming all armed at a great pace. 'Sir Knight,' saith he to Meliot, 'Can you tell me tidings of the Knight of the Galley?' 'What have you to do therein?' saith Meliot. 'Sir, the Lord of the Red Tower hath made bring Messire Gawain into a launde of this forest, and there, all unarmed, must he do battle with a lion. So my lord is waiting for the Knight of the Galley, that is to bring two damsels thither that the lion will devour when he shall have slain Messire Gawain.' 'Will the battle be presently?' saith Meliot. 'Yea, Sir,' saith the knight, 'Soon enough betimes, for Messire Gawain hath already been led thither and there bound to a stake until such time as the lion shall be come. Then will he be unbound, but even then two knights all armed will keep watch on him. But tell me tidings of the Knight of the Galley, and you have seen him?' 'Go forward,' saith he, 'and you will hear tidings of him.' Meliot departeth thereupon, a great gallop, and cometh nigh the launde whereunto Messire Gawain had been brought. He espied the two knights that kept guard over him, and if that Messire Gawain were in fear, little marvel was it, for he thought that his end had come. Meliot espied him bound to an iron staple with cords about the body on all sides so that he might not move. Meliot hath great pity thereof in his heart, and saith to himself that he will die there sooner than Messire Gawain shall die. He

clappeth spurs to his horse when he cometh **Meliot**
nigh the knights, and overtaketh one of them **rescueth**
with such a rush that he thrusteth his spear **Gawain**
right through his body, and beareth him down
dead.   The other was fain to go to the castle
for succour when he saw his fellow dead.
Meliot slew him forthwith. He cometh to
Messire Gawain, and so unbindeth him and
cutteth the cords wherewith he is bound. ' Sir,'
saith he, ' I am Meliot of Logres, your knight.'

V

When Messire Gawain felt himself unbound,
no need to ask whether he had joy thereof.
The tidings were come to the Red Court that
Queen Jandree was christened and baptized, and
that the Knight was come that had such force and
puissance in him that none might endure against
him for the God in whom he believed, and they
knew likewise that the Knight of the Galley
was dead, and Messire Gawain unbound and the
knights that guarded him slain.   They say that
there may they not abide, so they depart from
the castle and say that they will cross the sea to
protect their bodies, for that there they may
have no safety.

VI

When Meliot had delivered Messire Gawain
he made him be armed with the arms, such as
they were, of one of the knights he had slain.
Messire Gawain mounted on a horse such as
pleased him, and right great joy had he at heart.
They marvel much how it is that they of the
castle have not come after them, but they know

not their thought nor how they are scared. 'Meliot,' saith Messire Gawain, 'You have delivered me from death this time and one other, nor never had I acquaintance with any knight that hath done so much for me in so short a time as have you.' They departed the speediest they might and rode nigh enow to the castle, but they heard none moving within nor any noise, nor saw they none issue forth, and much marvelled they that none should come after them. They rode until they came to the head of the forest and caught sight of the sea, that was nigh enough before them, and saw that there was a great clashing of arms at the brink of the sea. A single knight was doing battle with all them that would fain have entered into a ship, and held stour so stiffly against them that he toppled the more part into the sea. They went thither as fast as they might, and when they drew nigh to the ship they knew that it was Perceval by his arms and his shield. Or ever they reached it, the ship was put off into the midst of the sea, wherein he was launched of his own great hardiment, and they went on fighting against him within the ship. 'Meliot,' saith Messire Gawain, 'See you, there is Perceval the Good Knight, and now may we say of a truth that he is in sore peril of death; for that ship, save God bethink Him thereof, shall arrive in such manner and in such a place as that never more shall we have no witting of him, and, so he perish for ever, no knight on live may have power to set forward the Law of our Lord.'

VII

Messire Gawain seeth the ship going further
away, and Perceval that defendeth himself
therein against them that set upon him. Right
heavy is he that he came not sooner, or ever the
ship had put off from the land. He turneth
back, he and Meliot together, and right sorrowful was Messire Gawain of Perceval, for they
knew not in what land he might arrive, and,
might he have followed, right gladly would he
have gone after him to aid him. They have
ridden until they meet a knight. Messire
Gawain asketh him whence he cometh, and
he saith from King Arthur's court. 'What
tidings can you tell us thereof?' saith Messire
Gawain. 'Sir, bad enough!' saith he. 'King
Arthur hath neglected all his knights for Briant
of the Isles, and hath put one of his best knights
in prison.' 'What is his name?' saith Messire
Gawain. 'Sir, he is called Lancelot of the
Lake. He had reconquered all the islands
that had been reft of King Arthur, and slain
King Madeglant, and conquered the land of
Oriande that he turned to the belief of the
Saviour of the World, and, so soon as he had
conquered his enemies, King Arthur sent for
him forthwith and straightway put him in his
prison by the counsel of Briant of the Isles.
But King Arthur will have a surfeit of friends
betimes; for King Claudas hath assembled his
folk in great plenty to reconquer the kingdom of
Oriande and come back upon King Arthur by
the counsel of Briant of the Isles that betrayeth

Arthur is blamed the King, for he hath made him his Seneschal and commander of all his land.'   ' Sir Knight,' saith Messire Gawain, 'Needs must the King miscarry that setteth aside the counsel of his good knights for the leasings of a traitor.'   Thereupon the knight departed from Messire Gawain. Right heavy is he of this that he hath said, that the King hath put Lancelot in prison.   Never tofore did he aught whereby he wrought so much to blame.

BRANCH XXXIV

TITLE I

HEREUPON the story is silent of Messire Gawain and Meliot, and speaketh of King Claudas that hath assembled a great folk by the counsel of Briant of the Isles to come into the land of King Arthur, for he knoweth that it is disgarnished of the good knights that wont there to be, and he knoweth all the secret plottings of the court and what power King Arthur hath withal. He draweth toward his land the nighest he may, and hath won back the kingdom of Oriande all at his will. But they of Albanie still hold against him and challenge the land the best they may. Tidings thereof come to the court of King Arthur, and they of the country send him word that so he send them not succour betimes they will yield up the land to King Claudas, and oftentimes they long after Lancelot, and say that so they had a defender like him, the islands would be all at peace. The King sent Briant of the Isles thither many times, that ever incontinent returned thence discomfit, but never sent he thither him that should have power to protect the land against King Claudas. King Arthur was sore troubled, for no witting had he of Messire Gawain nor Messire Ywain nor of others whereby his court had use of right to be feared and dreaded and

of high renown throughout all other kingdoms.
The King was one day in the hall at Cardoil,
right heavy; and he was at one of the windows,
and remembered him of the Queen and of his
good knights that he wont to see oftener at ·
court, whereof the more part were dead, and
of the adventures that wont to befall therein
whereof they saw none no longer. Lucan
the Butler seeth him right heavy and draweth
nigh to him quietly.

II

'Sir,' saith he, 'Meseemeth you are without
joy.' 'Lucan,' saith the King, 'Joy hath
been somewhat far from me sithence that the
Queen hath been dead, and Gawain and the
other knights have held aloof from my court so
that they deign come hither no longer. Moreover, King Claudas warreth upon me and con-
quereth my lands so that no power have I to
rescue me for default of my knights.' 'Sir,'
saith Lucan, 'Herein is there nought whereof
you have right to accuse any save yourself alone.
For you have done evil to him that hath served
you, and good to them that are traitors to you.
You have one of the best knights in the world
and the most loyal in your prison, wherefore all
the other hold them aloof from your court.
Lancelot had served you well by his good will
and by his good knighthood, nor never had he
done you any disservice whereof you might in
justice have done him such shame; nor never
will your enemies withhold them from you nor
have dread of you save only through him and

other your good knights. And know of a truth pleadeth
that Lancelot and Messire Gawain are the best for
of your court.' 'Lucan,' saith King Arthur, Lancelot
'So thought I ever again to have affiance in
him, I would make him be set forth of my
prison, for well I know that I have wrought
discourteously toward him; and Lancelot is of
a great heart, wherefore would he not slacken
of his despite for that which hath been done
unto him until such time as he should be avenged
thereof, for no king is there in the world, how
puissant soever he be, against whom he durst not
well maintain his right.'

III

'Sir,' saith Lucan, 'Lancelot well knoweth
that and you had taken no counsel but your
own, he would not have been thus entreated,
and I dare well say that never so long as he
liveth will he misdo in aught towards you, for
he hath in him much valour and loyalty, as
many a time have you had good cause to know.
Wherefore, and you would fain have aid and
succour and hold your realm again, behoveth
you set him forth of the prison, or otherwise
never will you succeed herein, and, if you do
not so, you will lose your land by treason.'
The King held by the counsel of Lucan the
Butler. He made bring Lancelot before him
into the midst of the hall, that was somewhat
made lean of his being in prison, but he bore
him as he wont, nor might none look at him
to whom he seemed not to be good knight.
'Lancelot,' saith the King, 'How is it with

you?'   'Sir,' saith he, 'It hath been ill with
me long time, but, please God, it shall be
better hereafter.'   'Lancelot,' saith the King,
'I repent me of this that I have done to you,
and I have bethought me much of the good
services I have found in you, wherefore I will
do you amends thereof at your will, in such
sort as that the love between us shall be whole
as it was tofore.'

IV

'Sir,' saith Lancelot, 'Your amends love I
much, and your love more than of any other;
but never, please God, will I misdo you for
aught that you may have done to me, for it is
well known that I have not been in prison for
no treason I have done, nor for no folly, but
only for that it was your will.   Never will it be
reproached me as of shame, and, sith that you
have done me nought whereof I may have
blame nor reproach, my devoir it is to withhold
me from hating you; for you are my lord, and
if that you do me ill, without flattery of myself
the ill you do me is your own; but, please
God, whatsoever you have done me, never shall
my aid fail you, rather, everywhere will I set
my body in adventure for your love, in like
sort as I have done many a time.'

V

In the court of King Arthur was right great
joy of the most part when they heard that
Lancelot was set forth of prison, but not a

whit rejoiced were Briant and his folk. The **Briant** King commanded that Lancelot should be well **fain to** cared for and made whole again, and that all **depart** should be at his commandment. The court was all overjoyed thereof, and they said: now at last might the King make war in good assurance. Lancelot was foremost in the King's court and more redoubted than was ever another of the knights. Briant of the Isles came one day before the King. 'Sir,' saith he, 'Behold, here is Lancelot that wounded me in your service, wherefore I will that he know I am his enemy.' 'Briant,' saith Lancelot, 'And if that you deserved it tofore, well may you be sorry thereof, and sith that you wish to be mine enemy, your friend will I not be. For well may I deem of your love according as I have found it in you.' 'Sir,' saith Briant to the King, 'You are my lord, and I am one you are bound to protect. You know well that so rich am I in lands and so puissant in friends that I may well despise mine enemy, nor will I not remain at your court so long as Lancelot is therein. Say not that I depart thence with any shame as toward myself. Rather thus go I hence as one that will gladly avenge me, so I have place and freedom, and I see plainly and know that you and your court love him far better than you love me, wherefore behoveth me take thought thereof.' 'Briant,' saith the King, 'Remain as yet, and I will make amends for you to Lancelot, and I myself will make amends for him to you.'

VI

'Sir,' saith Briant, 'By the faith that I owe
to you, none amends will I have of him nor
other until such time as I have drawn as much
blood of his body as did he of mine, and I
will well that he know it.' With that Briant
departeth from the court all wrathful, but if
that Lancelot had not feared to anger the
King, Briant would not have ridden a league
English or ever he had followed and forced
him to fight. Briant goeth toward the Castle
of the Hard Rock, and saith that better would
it have been for the King that Lancelot were
still in prison, for that such a plea will he move
against him and he may bring it to bear, as that
he shall lose thereof the best parcel of his land.
He is gone into the land of King Claudas, and
saith that now at last hath he need of his aid,
for Lancelot is issued forth of the King's
prison and is better loved at court than all
other, so that the King believeth in no counsel
save his only. King Claudas sweareth to him
and maketh pledge that never will he fail him,
and Briant to him again.

BRANCH XXXV

TITLE I

HEREWITHAL is the story silent of Perceval Briant and talketh of Perceval, that the ship beareth away right swiftly; but so long hath he held battle therein that every one hath he slain of them that were in the ship save only the pilot that steereth her, for him hath he in covenant that he will believe in God and renounce his evil Law. Perceval is far from land so that he seeth nought but sea only, and the ship speedeth onward, and God guideth him, as one that believeth in Him and loveth Him and serveth Him of a good heart. The ship ran on by night and by day as it pleased God, until that they saw a castle and an island of the sea. He asked his pilot if he knew what castle it was. 'Certes,' saith he, 'Not I, for so far have we run that I know not neither the sea nor the stars.' They come nigh the castle, and saw four that sounded bells at the four corners of the town, right sweetly, and they that sounded them were clad in white garments. They are come thither.

II

So soon as the ship had taken haven under the castle, the sea withdraweth itself back, so that the ship is left on dry land. None were

Perceval
seeth

therein save Perceval, his horse, and the pilot.
They issued forth of the ship and went by the
side of the sea toward the castle, and therein
were the fairest halls and the fairest mansions
that any might see ever. He looketh under-
neath a tree that was tall and broad and seeth
the fairest fountain and the clearest that any
may devise, and it was all surrounded of rich
pillars, and the gravel thereof seemed to be
gold and precious stones. Above this fountain
were two men sitting, their beards and hair
whiter than driven snow, albeit they seemed
young of visage. So soon as they saw Perceval
they dressed them to meet him, and bowed
down and worshipped the shield that he bare
at his neck, and kissed the cross and then the
boss wherein were the hallows. 'Sir,' say
they, 'Marvel not of this that we do, for well
knew we the knight that bare this shield tofore
you. Many a time we saw him or ever God
were crucified.' Perceval marvelleth much of
this that they say, for they talk of a time that
is long agone.

III

'Lords, know ye then how he was named?'
Say they, 'Joseph of Abarimacie, but no cross
was there on the shield before the death of
Jesus Christ. But he had it set thereon after
the crucifixion of Jesus Christ for the sake of
the Saviour that he loved so well.' Perceval
took off the shield from his neck, and one of
the worshipful men setteth upon it as it were
a posy of herbs that was blooming with the

fairest flowers in the world.   Perceval looketh **many**
beyond the fountain and seeth in a right fair **marvels**
place a round vessel like as it were ivory, and
it was so large that there was a knight within,
all armed.   He looketh thereinto and seeth the
knight, and speaketh to him many times, but
never the more willeth the knight to answer
him.   Perceval looketh at him in wonderment,
and cometh back to the good men and asketh
them who is this knight, and they tell him that
he may know not as yet.   They lead him to
a great hall and bear his shield before him,
whereof they make right great joy, and show
thereunto great worship.   He seeth the hall
right rich, for hall so rich and so fair had he
seen never.   It was hung about with right rich
cloths of silk, and in the midst of the hall was
imaged the Saviour of the World so as He is in
His majesty, with the apostles about Him, and
within were great galleries that were full of
folk and seemed to be of great holiness, and so
were they, for had they not been good men
they might not there have remained.

VI

'Sir,' say the two Masters to Perceval,
'This house that you see here so rich, is the
hall royal.'   'By my faith,' saith Perceval,
'So ought it well to be, for never saw I none
so much of worth.'   He looketh all around, and
seeth the richest tables of gold and ivory that
he saw ever.   One of the Masters clappeth his
hands thrice, and three and thirty men come
into the hall all in a company.   They were clad

in white garments, and not one of them but had
a red cross in the midst of his breast, and they
seemed to be all of an age. As soon as they
enter into the hall they do worship to God Our
Lord and set out their cups.   Then went they
to wash at a great laver of gold, and then went
to sit at the tables. The Masters made Perceval
sit at the most master-table with themselves.
They were served thereat right gloriously, and
Perceval looked about him more gladlier than
he ate.

V

And while he was thus looking, he seeth a
chain of gold come down above him loaded
with precious stones, and in the midst thereof
was a crown of gold. The chain descended
a great length and held on to nought save to the
will of Our Lord only. As soon as the Masters
saw it descending they opened a great wide pit
that was in the midst of the hall, so that one
could see the hole all openly. As soon as the
entrance of this pit was discovered, there issued
thence the greatest cry and most dolorous that
any heard ever, and when the worshipful men
hear it, they stretched out their hands towards
Our Lord and all began to weep. Perceval
heareth this dolour, and marvelleth much what
it may be. He seeth that the chain of gold
descendeth thither and is there stayed until they
have well-nigh eaten, and then draweth itself
again into the air and so goeth again aloft. But
Perceval knoweth not what became thereof, and
the Master covereth the pit again, that was right

grisly to see, and pitiful to hear were the voices **Perceval** that issued therefrom. **his** **promise**

VI

The Good Men rose from the tables when they had eaten, and gave thanks right sweetly to Our Lord; and then returned thither whence they had come. 'Sir,' saith the Master to Perceval, 'The chain of gold that you have seen is right precious and the crown of gold likewise. But never may you issue forth from hence save you promise to return so soon as you shall see the ship and the sail crossed of a red cross; otherwise may you not depart hence.' 'Tell me,' saith he, 'of the chain of gold and the crown, what it may be?' 'We will tell you not,' saith one of the Masters, 'save you promise that which I tell you.' 'Certes, Sir,' saith Perceval, 'I promise you faithfully, that so soon as I shall have done that I have to do for my lady my mother and one other, that I will return hither, so I be on live and I see your ship so marked as you say.' 'Yea, be you faithful to the end herein, and you shall have the crown of gold upon your head so soon as you return, and so shall you be seated in the throne, and shall be king of an island that is near to this, right plenteous of all things good, for nought is there in the world that is there lacking that is needful for man's body. King Hermit was the king thereof that thus hath garnished it, and for that he approved himself so well in this kingdom, and that they who are in the island consented thereto, is he chosen to be

Plenteous king of a greater realm.   Now they desire that
Island another worshipful man be sent them for king,
that shall do for them as much good as did he,
but take you good heed, sith that you will be
king therein, that the island be well garnished;
for, and you garnish it not well, you will be
put into the Poverty-stricken Island, the crying
whereof you have but now since heard, and the
crown thereof will again be reft from you.
For they that have been kings of the Plenteous
Island and have not well approved them, are
among the folk that you saw in the Poverty-
stricken Island, lacking in all things good.   And
so I tell you that King Hermit, whom you
will succeed, hath sent thither a great part of
his folk.   There are the heads sealed in silver,
and the heads sealed in lead, and the bodies
whereunto these heads belonged; I tell you
that you must make come thither the head both
of the King and of the Queen.   But of the
other I tell you that they are in the Poverty-
stricken Island.   But we know not whether
they shall ever issue forth thence.'

VII

'Sir,' saith Perceval, 'Tell me of the knight
that is all armed in the ivory vessel, who he is,
and what is the name of this castle?'   'You
may not know,' saith the Master, 'until your
return.   But tell me tidings of the most Holy
Graal, that you reconquered, is it still in the
holy chapel that was King Fisherman's?'
'Yea, Sir,' saith Perceval, 'And the sword

wherewith S. John was beheaded, and other hallows in great plenty.' 'I saw the Graal,' saith the Master, 'or ever Joseph, that was uncle to King Fisherman, collected therein the blood of Jesus Christ. Know that well am I acquainted with all your lineage, and of what folk you were born. For your good knighthood and for your good cleanness and for your good valour came you in hither, for such was Our Lord's will, and take heed that you be ready when place shall be, and time shall come, and you shall see the ship apparelled.' 'Sir,' saith Perceval, 'Most willingly shall I return, nor never would I have sought to depart but for my lady my mother, and for my sister, for never have I seen no place that so much hath pleased me.' He was right well harboured the night within, and in the morning, or ever he departed, heard a holy mass in a holy chapel the fairest that he had seen ever. The Master cometh to him after the mass and bringeth him a shield as white as snow. Afterwards, he saith, 'You will leave me your shield within for token of your coming and will bear this.' 'Sir,' saith Perceval, 'I will do your pleasure.' He hath taken leave, and so departeth from the rich mansion, and findeth the ship all apparelled, and heareth sound the bells at his forth-going the same as at his coming. He entereth into the ship and the sail is set. He leaveth the land far behind, and the pilot steereth the ship and Our Lord God guideth and leadeth him. The ship runneth a great speed, for far enough had she to run, but God made her speed as He

A poor
castle would, for He knew the passing great goodness and worth of the knight that was within.

VIII

God hath guided and led the ship by day and by night until that she arrived at an island where was a castle right ancient, but it seemed not to be over-rich, rather it showed as had it been of great lordship in days of yore. They cast anchor, and Perceval is come toward the castle and entereth in all armed. He seeth the castle large, and the dwelling-chambers fallen down and the house-place roofless, and he seeth a lady sitting before the steps of an old hall. She rose up as soon as she saw him, but she was right poorly clad. It seemed well by her body and her cheer and her bearing that she was a gentlewoman, and he seeth that two damsels come with her that are young of age and are as poorly clad as is the lady. 'Sir,' saith she to Perceval, 'Welcome may you be. No knight have I seen enter this castle of a long time.' 'Lady,' saith Perceval, 'God grant you joy and honour!' 'Sir,' saith she, 'Need have we thereof, for none scarce have I had this long while past.' She leadeth him into a great ancient hall that was right poorly garnished. 'Sir,' saith she, 'Here will you harbour you the night, and you would take in good part that we may do and you knew the plight of this castle.' She maketh him be unarmed of a servant that was there within, and the damsels come before him and serve him right sweetly. The lady bringeth him a mantle to do on.

'Sir,' saith she, 'Within are no better garments The lady
wherewith to show you honour than this.' thereof
Perceval looketh on the damsels and hath great
pity of them, for so well shapen were they
of limb and body as that nature might not have
better fashioned them, and all the beauty that
may be in woman's body was in them, and all
the sweetness and simpleness.

IX

'Lady,' saith Perceval, 'Is this castle, then,
not yours?' 'Sir,' saith she, 'So much is all
that remaineth to me of all my land, and you
see there my daughters of whom is it right sore
pity, for nought have they but what you see,
albeit gentlewomen are they and of high lineage,
but their kinsfolk are too far away, and a knight
that is right cruel hath reft us of our land
sithence that my lord was dead, and holdeth a
son of mine in his prison, whereof I am right
sorrowful, for he is one of the comeliest knights
in the world. He had not been knight more
than four years when he took him, and now
may I aid neither myself nor other, but I have
heard tell that there is a knight in the land of
Wales that was the son of Alain li Gros of the
Valleys of Camelot, and he is the Best Knight
in the World, and this Alain was brother of
Calobrutus, whose wife was I, and of whom I
had my son and these two daughters. This
know I well, that and the Good Knight that
is so near akin to them were by any adventure
to come into this island, I should have my son
again, and my daughters that are disherited

would have their lands again freely, and so should I be brought out of sore pain and poverty. I am of another lineage that is full far away, for King Ban of Benoic that is dead was mine uncle, but he hath a son that is a right good knight as I have been told, so that and one of these two should come nigh me in any of these islands right joyous should I be thereof.'

X

Perceval heareth that the two damsels are his uncle's daughters, and hath great pity thereof. 'Lady,' saith he, 'How is he named that is in prison?' 'Sir,' saith she, 'Galobruns, and he that holdeth him in prison is named Gohaz of the Castle of the Whale.' 'Is his castle near this, Lady?' saith he. 'Sir, there is but an arm of the sea to cross, and in all these islands of the sea is there none that hath any puissance but he only, and so assured is he that no dread hath he of any. For none that is in this land durst offend against him. Sir, one thing hath he bid me do, whereof I am sore grieved, that and I send him not one of my daughters, he hath sworn his oath that he will reave me of my castle.' 'Lady,' saith Perceval, 'An oath is not always kept. To the two damsels, please God, shall he do no shame, and right heavy am I of that he hath done already, for they were daughters of mine uncle. Alain li Gros was my father and Galobrutus my uncle, and many another good man that now is dead.'

XI

When the damsels heard this, they kneeled
down before him, and began to weep for joy
and kiss his hands, and pray him for God's sake
have mercy on them and on their brother.
And he saith that he will not depart from their
land until he hath done all he may.   He remaineth the night in the castle and his mariner
likewise.   The lady made great joy of Perceval,
and did him all the honour she might.   When
the morrow came they showed him the land of
the King that had reft them of their land, but
the lady could not tell him where her son was
in prison.   He departeth and cometh back to
his ship when he hath taken leave of the lady
and the damsels, and right glad was he to know
that the damsels were so nigh to him of kin.
So he prayeth God grant him that he may be
able to give them back their land and bring
them out of the poverty wherein they are.   He
roweth until that he is come under a rock,
wherein was a cave at top round and narrow
and secure like as it were a little house.
Perceval looketh on that side, and seeth a man
sitting within.   He maketh the ship draw nigh
the rock, then looketh and seeth the cutting of
a way that went upwards through the rock.
He is come forth of the ship and goeth up the
little path until he cometh into the little house.
He findeth within one of the comeliest knights
in the world.   He had a ring at his feet and
a collar on his neck with a chain whereof the
other end was fixed by a staple into a great

Galo- ledge of the rock. He rose up over against
bruns in Perceval as soon as he saw him. 'Sir Knight,'
prison saith Perceval, 'You are well made fast.' 'Sir,
that irketh me,' saith the knight; 'Better should
I like myself elsewhere than here.' 'You
would be right,' saith Perceval, 'For you are in
right evil plight in the midst of this sea. Have
you aught within to eat or to drink?' 'Sir,'
saith he, 'The daughter of the Sick Knight that
dwelleth in the island hard by, sendeth me every
day in a boat as much meat as I may eat, for
she hath great pity of me. The King that hath
imprisoned me here hath reft her castles like
as he hath those of my lady my mother.'
'May none remove you hence?' 'Sir, in no
wise, save he that set me here, for he keepeth
with him the key of the lock, and he told me
when he departed hence that never more should
I issue forth.' 'By my head,' saith Perceval,
'but you shall! And you were the son of
Galobrutus, you were the son of mine uncle,'
saith Perceval, 'and I of yours, so that it
would be a reproach to me for evermore and
I left you in this prison.'

XII

When Galobruns heareth that he is his
uncle's son, great joy hath he thereof. He
would have fallen at his feet, but Perceval
would not, and said to him, 'Now be well
assured, for I will seek your deliverance.' He
cometh down from the rock, and so entereth
the ship and roweth of a long space. He
looketh before him and seeth a right rich island

and a right plenteous, and on the other side he **Gohaz**
seeth in a little islet a knight that is mounted **in a tree**
up in a tall tree that was right broad with many
boughs. There was a damsel with him, that
had climbed up also for dread of a serpent,
great and evil-favoured, that had issued from
a hole in a mountain. The damsel seeth
Perceval's ship coming, and crieth out to him.
'Ha, Sir,' saith she, 'Come to help this King
that is up above, and me that am a damsel!'
'Whereof are you afeard, damsel?' saith
Perceval. 'Of a great serpent, Sir,' saith she,
'that hath made us climb up, whereof ought I
not to be sorry, for this King hath carried me
off from my father's house, and would have
done me shame of my body and this serpent
had not run upon him.' 'And what is the
King's name, damsel?' saith Perceval. 'Sir,
he is called Gohaz of the Castle of the Whale.
This great land is his own that is so plenteous,
and other lands enow that he hath reft of my
father and of other.' The King had great
shame of this that the damsel told him, and
made answer never a word. Perceval understandeth that it was he that held his cousin in
prison, and is issued from the ship forthwith,
sword drawn. The serpent seeth him, and
cometh toward him, jaws yawning, and casteth
forth fire and flame in great plenty. Perceval
thrusteth his sword right through the gullet.
'Now may you come down,' saith he to the
King. 'Sir,' saith he, 'The key of a chain
wherewith a certain knight is bound hath
fallen, and the serpent seized it.' Perceval

rendeth open the throat and findeth the key forthwith, all red-hot with the fire of the serpent. The King cometh down, that hath no dread of aught, but cometh, rather, as he ought, to thank Perceval of the goodness he had done him, and Perceval seizeth him between his arms and beareth him away to the ship.

XIII

'Sir Knight,' saith Gohaz, 'Take heed what you do, for I am King of this land.' 'Therefore,' saith Perceval, 'I do it. For, had it been another I should do it not.' 'Ha, Sir,' saith the damsel, 'Leave me not here to get forth as I may, but help me until that I shall be in the house of my father, the Sick Knight, that is sore grieved on my account.' Perceval understandeth that it is the damsel of whom Galobruns spake such praise. He goeth to bring her down from the tree, then bringeth her into the ship, and so goeth back toward the rock where his cousin was. 'Sir Knight,' saith Gohaz, 'Where will you put me?' 'I will put you,' saith he, 'as an enemy, there, where you have put the son of mine uncle in prison; so shall I avenge me of you, and he also at his will.' When the King heard this, he was glad thereof not a whit, and the damsel was loath not a whit, whom he had thus disherited. They row until they come to the rock. Perceval issueth forth of the ship, and bringeth Gohaz up maugre his head. Galobruns seeth him coming and maketh great joy thereof, and Perceval saith to him: 'Behold here your

mortal enemy! Now do your will of him!'
He taketh the key and so looseth him of the
irons wherein he was imprisoned.

XIV

'Galobruns,' saith Perceval, 'Now may you
do your pleasure of your enemy?' 'Sir,' saith
he, 'Right gladly!' He maketh fast the irons
on his feet that he had upon his own, and
afterward setteth the collar on his neck. 'Now
let him be here,' saith he, 'in such sort and in
such prison as he put me; for well I know that
he will be succoured of none.' After that, he
flingeth the key into the sea as far as he might,
and so seemed it to Galobruns that he well
avenged himself in such wise, and better than if
he had killed him. Perceval alloweth him
everything therein at his will. They enter into
the ship and leave Gohaz all sorrowing on the
rock, that never thereafter ate nor drank. And
Perceval bringeth his cousin and the damsel,
and they row until that they come into their
land, and Perceval maketh send for all the folk
of King Gohaz and maketh all the more
powerful do sure homage to Galobruns and his
sisters in such sort that the land was all at their
will. He sojourned there so long as it pleased
him, and then departed and took leave of the
damsel and Galobruns, that thanked him much
for the lands that he had again through him.

XV

Perceval hath rowed until that he is come
nigh a castle that was burning fiercely with a
great flame, and seeth a hermitage upon the sea

King hard by. He seeth the hermit at the door of
Hermit's the chapel, and asketh him what the castle is
castle that hath caught fire thus.   'Sir,' saith the
hermit, 'I will tell you. Joseus, the son of
King Pelles, slew his mother there.   Never
sithence hath the castle stinted of burning, and
I tell you that of this castle and one other will
be kindled the fire that shall burn up the world
and put it to an end.'   Perceval marvelleth
much, and knew well that it was the castle of
King Hermit his uncle.   He departeth thence
in great haste, and passeth three kingdoms and
saileth by the wastes and deserts on one side
and the other of the sea, for the ship ran somewhat a-nigh the land.   He looketh and seeth on
an island twelve hermits sitting on the sea-shore.
The sea was calm and untroubled, and he made
cast the anchor so as to keep the ship steady.
Then he saluteth the hermits, and they all bow
down to him in answer.   He asketh them
where have they their repair, and they tell him
that they have not far away twelve chapels
and twelve houses that surround a grave-yard
wherein lie twelve dead knights that we keep
watch over.   They were all brothers-german,
and right worshipful men, and none thereof lived
more than twelve years knight save one only,
and none of them was there but won much land
and broad kingdoms from the misbelievers, and
they all died in arms ; and the name of the
eldest was Alain li Gros, and he came into this
country from the Valleys of Camelot to avenge
his brother Alibans of the Waste City that the
Giant King had slain, and he took vengeance on

him thereof, but he died thereafter of a wound **The**
that the Giant had given him. 'Sir,' saith **twelve**
one of the hermits, 'I was at his death, but **tombs**
nought was there he so longed after as a son
of his, and he said that his name was Perceval.
He was the last of the brothers that died.'

XVI

When Perceval heard this he had pity
thereof, and issued forth of the ship and came to
land, and his mariner with him. He prayed the
hermits that they would lead him to the grave-
yard where the knights lay, and gladly did they
so. Perceval is come thither and seeth the
coffins right rich and fair, and the chapels full
fairly dight, and every coffin lay over against
the altar in each chapel. 'Lords, which
coffin is that of the Lord of Camelot?' 'This,
the highest,' say the hermits, 'and the most
rich, for that he was eldest of all the brethren.'
Perceval kneeleth down before it, then embraceth the coffin and prayeth right sweetly for
the soul of his father, and in like manner he
went to all the other coffins. He harboured
the night with the hermits, and told them that
Alain li Gros was his father and all the other
his uncles. Right joyous were the hermits for
that he was come thither, and the morrow, or
ever he departed, he heard mass in the chapel of
his father and in the others where he might.
He entered into the ship and sped full swift,
and so far hath the ship run that he draweth
nigh the islands of Great Britain. He arriveth
at the head of a forest under the Red Tower

whereof he had slain the lord, there where
Meliot delivered Messire Gawain. He is
issued forth of the ship and leadeth forth his
horse and is armed, and commendeth the pilot
to God. He mounteth on his destrier, all
armed, and goeth amidst the land that was
well-nigh void of people, for he himself had
slain the greater part thereof, albeit he knew it
not. He rideth so long, right amidst the
country, that he cometh toward evensong to a
hold that was in a great forest, and he bethought
him that he would go into the hermitage, and
he cometh straight into the hold, and seeth a
knight lying in the entrance of the gate on a
straw mattress, and a damsel sate at the bed's
head, of passing great beauty, and held his head
on her lap.

XVII

The knight reviled her from time to time,
and said that he would make cut off her head
and he had not that he desired to have, for that
he was sick. Perceval looked at the lady that
held him and served him full sweetly, and
deemed her to be a good lady and a loyal.
The Sick Knight called to Perceval. 'Sir,'
saith he, 'Are you come in hither to harbour?'
'Sir,' saith Perceval, 'So please you, I will
harbour here.' 'Then blame me not,' saith
the knight, 'of that you shall see me do to my
wife.' 'Sir,' saith Perceval, 'Sith that she is
yours, you have a right to do your pleasure,
but in all things ought one to be heedful on one's
way.' The knight made him be carried back

into the dwelling, for that he had been in the air and his
as long as pleased him, and commandeth his wife
wife that she do much honour to the knight that
is come to lodge within. 'But take heed,'
saith he, 'that you be not seen at the table, but
eat, as you are wont, at the squire's table, for,
until such time as I have the golden cup I
desire, I will not forgo my despite against you.'

XVIII

Perceval unarmed him. The lady had
brought him a surcoat of scarlet for him to do
on, and he asked her wherefore her lord reviled
her and rebuked her in such sort, and she told
him all the story how Lancelot had married her
to him, and how her lord ever sithence had
dishonoured her. 'Sir,' saith she, 'Now hath
he fallen into misease, sithence then, and he
hath a brother as sick as he is, and therefore
hath Gohaz of the Castle of the Whale reft him
of his land, whereof is he right sorry, and my
lord hath never been heal since that he heard
thereof. And well you know that such folk
wax wroth of a little, and are overjoyed when
they have a little thing that pleaseth them, for
they live always in desire of somewhat. My
lord hath heard tell of a cup of gold that a
damsel beareth, that is right rich and of greater
worth than aught he hath seen this long time,
and a knight goeth with the damsel that beareth
the cup, and saith that none may have it save
he be the Best Knight in the World. My lord
hath told me many times, sithence he heard
tidings thereof, that never shall the despite he

An hath toward me be forgone, until that he shall
assembly have the cup.   But he is so angry withal with
his brother that hath lost his land, that I aby it
right dear, for I do all his will and yet may I
have no fair treatment of him.   Howbeit, for
no ill that he may do, nor no churlishness that
he may say, will I be against him in nought
that he hath set his mind on.   For I would
have him, and I had him, blessed be Lancelot
through whom it was so.   As much as I loved
him in health, so much love I him in his sickness, and more yet, for I desire to deserve that
God shall bring him to a better mind.'

XIX

'Lady,' saith Perceval, 'Great praise ought
you to have of this that you say; but you may
well tell him of a truth that the sick King his
brother hath all his land freely and his daughter, for I was at the reconquering thereof, and
know the knight well that gave it back to him.
But of the golden cup can I give you no witting.'
'Sir,' saith she, 'The damsel is to bear it to an
assembly of knights that is to be held hard by
this, under the White Tower.   There hath she
to give it to the best knight, and him that shall
do best at the assembly, and the knight that
followeth the damsel is bound to carry it whither
he that shall win it may command, and if he
would fain it should be given to another rather
than to himself.'   'Lady,' saith Perceval,
'Well meseemeth that he who shall win the
cup by prize of arms will be right courteous and
he send it to you, and God grant that he that

hath it may do you such bounty as you desire.' **at the**
'Sir,' saith she, 'Methinketh well, so Lancelot **White**
were there, either he or Messire Gawain, that, **Tower**
and they won it, so they remembered them of
me, and knew how needful it were to me, they
would promise me the cup.' 'Lady,' saith
Perceval, 'By one of these twain ought you
well to have it, for greater prize now long since
have they won.' She goeth to her lord and
saith to him : 'Sir,' saith she, 'Now may you
be more joyous than is your wont, for that your
brother hath his land again all quit. For the
knight that is within was at the reconquering.'
The Sick Knight heard her and had great joy
thereof. 'Go!' saith he to his wife, 'and do
great honour to the knight, but take heed you
sit not otherwise than you are wont.' 'Sir,'
saith she, 'I will not.'

XX

The damsel maketh Perceval sit at meat.
When he had washen, he thought that the lady
should have come to sit beside him, but she
would not disobey her lord's commandment.
When Perceval was set at the table and he had
been served of the first meats, thereupon the lady
went to sit with the squires. Perceval was much
shamed that she should sit below, but he was not
minded to speak, for she had told him somewhat
of her lord's manner. Howbeit, he lay the
night in the hold, and, on the morrow when he
had taken leave, he departed, and bethought
him in his courage that the knight would do
good chivalry and great alms that should do this

sick knight his desire as concerning the cup, in such sort as that his wife should be freed of the annoy that she is in, for that all knights that knew thereof ought to have pity of her. Perceval goeth his way as he that hath great desire to accomplish that he hath to do, and to see the token of his going again to the castle where the chain of gold appeared to him, for never yet saw he dwelling that pleased him so much. He hath ridden so far that he is come into the joyless forest of the Black Hermit, that is so loathly and horrible that no leaves nor greenery are there by winter nor by summer, nor was song of bird never heard therein, but all the land is gruesome and burnt, and wide are the cracks therein. He hath scarce gone thereinto or ever he hath overtaken the Damsel of the Car, that made full great joy of him. 'Sir,' saith she, 'Bald was I the first time I saw you; now may you see that I have my hair.' 'Certes, yea!' saith Perceval, 'And, as methinketh, hair passing beautiful.' 'Sir,' saith she, 'I was wont to carry my arm at my neck in a scarf of gold and silk, for that I thought the service I did you in the hostel of King Fisherman your uncle had been ill bestowed; but now well I see that it was not; wherefore now carry I the one arm in the same manner as the other; and the damsel that wont to go a-foot now goeth a-horseback; and blessed be you that have so approved you in goodness by the good manner of your heart, and by your likeness to the first of your lineage, whom you resemble in all good conditions. Sir,' saith she, 'I durst not come nigh the castle, for there be archers there that shoot so **Black** sore that none may endure their strokes, and **Hermit's** hereof will they stint not, they say, until such **Castle** time as you be come thither. But well know I wherefore they will cease then, for they will come to shut you up within to slay and to destroy. Natheless all they that are within will have no power, nor will they do you evil, save only the lord of the castle ; but he will do battle against you right gladly.'

XXI

Perceval goeth toward the castle of the Black Hermit, and the Damsel of the Car after. The archers draw and shoot stoutly. Perceval goeth forward a great gallop, but they know him not on account of the white shield. They think rather that it is one of the other knights, and they lodge many arrows in his shield. He came nigh a drawbridge over a moat right broad and foul and horrible, and the bridge was lowered so soon as he came, and all the archers left of shooting. Then knew they well that it was Perceval who came. The door was opened to receive him, for they of the gate and they of the castle within thought to have power to slay him. But so soon as they saw him, they lost their will thereof and were all amated and without strength, and said that they would set this business on their lord that was strong enough and puissant enough to slay one man. Perceval entered all armed into a great hall, and found it filled all around with a great throng of folk that

was right foul to look on.   He that was called
the Black Hermit was full tall and seemed to
be of noble lordship, and he was in the midst of
the hall, all armed.   'Sir,' say his men, 'And
you have not defence of yourself, never no
counsel nor aid may you have of us!

XXII

'We are yours to guard, to protect, and
oftentimes have we defended you; now defend
us in this sore need.'   The Black Hermit sate
upon a tall black horse, and was right richly
armed.   So soon as Perceval espieth him, he
cometh with such a rush against him that he
maketh all the hall resound, and the Black
Hermit cometh in like sort.   They mell together with such force that the Black Hermit
breaketh his spear upon Perceval, but Perceval
smiteth him so passing stoutly on the left side
upon the shield, that he beareth him to the
ground beside his horse, so that in the fall he
made he to-frushed two of the great ribs in the
overturn.   And when they that were therein
saw him fall, they opened the trap-door of a
great pit that was in the midst of the hall.   So
soon as they had opened it, the foulest stench
that any smelt ever issued thereout.   They
take their lord and cast him into this abysm
and this filth.   After that, they come to
Perceval, and so yield the castle and put them
at his mercy in everything.   Thereupon, behold
you, the Damsel of the Car that cometh.   They
deliver up to her the heads sealed in gold, both

the head of the King and of the Queen, and **The** she departeth forthwith, for well knoweth she **golden** that Perceval will achieve that he hath to do **cup** without her. She departeth from the castle and goeth the speediest she may toward the Valleys of Camelot. And all they of the castle that had been the Black Hermit's are obedient to Perceval to do his will, and they have him in covenant that never more shall knights be harassed there in such sort as they had been theretofore, but rather that they should receive gladly any knights that should pass that way, like as in other places. Perceval departed from the castle rejoicing for that he had drawn them to the believe of Our Lord, and every day was His service done therein in holy wise, like as it is done in other places.

XXIII

Hereof ought the good knight to be loved that by the goodness of his heart and the loyalty of his knighthood hath achieved all the emprises he undertook, without reproach and without blame. Perceval hath ridden until he hath overtaken the damsel that carried the rich cup of gold and the knight that was along with her. Perceval saluteth him, and the knight maketh answer, may he be blessed of God and of His sweet Mother. 'Fair Sir,' saith Perceval, 'Is this damsel of your company?' Saith the knight, 'Rather am I of hers. But we are going to an assembly of knights that is to be under the White Tower to the intent to

Perceval prove which knight is most worth, and to him
winneth that shall have the prize of the assembly shall
be delivered this golden cup.' 'By my head,'
saith Perceval, 'That will be fair to see!'
He departeth from the knight and the damsel,
and goeth his way a great pace amidst the
meadows under the White Tower, whither
the knights were coming from all parts, and
many of them were already armed to issue
forth. So soon as it was known that the
damsel with the cup was come thither, the
fellowships assembled on all sides, and great was
the clashing of arms. Perceval hurleth into
the assembly in such sort that many a knight
he smiteth down and overthroweth at his
coming, and he giveth so many blows and so
many receiveth that all they that behold marvel
much how he may abide. The assembly lasted
until evensong, and when it came to an end the
damsel came to the knights and prayed and
required that they would declare to her by
right judgment of arms which had done the
best. The more part said that he of the white
shield had surpassed them all in arms, and all
agreed thereto. The damsel was right glad,
for well she knew that they spake truth. She
cometh to Perceval; 'Sir,' saith she, 'I present
you this cup of gold for your good chivalry,
and therefore is it meet and right you should
know whence the cup cometh. The elder
Damsel of the Tent where the evil custom was
wont to be, sent it to Messire Gawain, and
Messire Gawain made much joy thereof. And
it came to pass on such wise that Brundans, the

son of the sister of Briant of the Isles, slew **the golden cup** Meliot of Logres, the most courteous knight and the most valiant that was in the realm of Logres, and thereof was Messire Gawain so sorrowful that he knew not how to contain himself. For Meliot had twice rescued him from death, and King Arthur once. He was liegeman of Messire Gawain. Wherefore he prayeth and beseecheth you on his behalf that you receive not the cup save you undertake to avenge him. For he was loved of all the court, albeit he had haunted it but little. Brundans slew him in treason when Meliot was unawares of him.' 'Damsel,' saith Perceval, 'Were there no cup at all, yet natheless should I be fain to do the will of Messire Gawain, for never might I love the man that had deserved his hatred.' He taketh the cup in his hand. 'Damsel,' saith he, 'I thank you much hereof, and God grant I may reward you for the same.' 'Sir,' saith she, 'Brundans is a right proud knight, and beareth a shield party of vert and argent. He is minded never to change his cognisance, for that his father bore the same.' Perceval called the knight that was of the damsel's company. 'I beseech you,' saith he, 'of guerdon and of service, that you bear this cup for me to the hold of the Sick Knight, and tell his wife that the Knight of the White Shield that was harboured there within hath sent it her by you.' 'Sir,' saith the knight, 'This will I do gladly to fulfil your will.' He taketh the cup to furnish out the conditions of the message, and so departeth forthwith.

XXIV

Perceval lay the night in the castle of the
White Tower, and departed thence on the
morrow as he that would fain do somewhat
whereof he might deserve well of Messire
Gawain. Many a time had he heard tell of
Meliot of Logres and of his chivalry and of
his great valour. He was entered into a forest,
and had heard mass of a hermit, from whom he
had departed. He came to the Castle Perilous
that was hard by there where Meliot lay sick,
lay wounded, when Lancelot brought him the
sword and the cloth wherewith he touched his
wounds. He entered into the castle and
alighted. The damsel of the castle, that made
great dole, came to meet Perceval. 'Damsel,'
saith he, 'Wherefore are you so sorrowful?'
'Sir,' saith she, 'For a knight that I tended
and healed herewithin, whom Brundans hath
killed in treason, and God thereof grant us
vengeance yet, for so courteous knight saw I
never.' While she was speaking in this manner,
forthwith behold you a damsel that cometh.
'Ha, Sir!' saith she to Perceval, 'Mount you
again and come to aid us, for none other knight
find I in this land nor in this forest but only
you all alone!' 'What need have you of my
aid?' saith Perceval. 'A knight is carrying
off my lady by force, that was going to the
court of King Arthur.' 'Who is your lady?'
saith Perceval. 'Sir, she is the younger
Damsel of the Tent where Messire Gawain
overthrew the evil customs. For God's sake,

hasten you, for he revileth her sore for her love **Brundans**
of the King and of Messire Gawain.' Perceval **boasteth**
remounteth forthwith and issueth forth of the
castle on the spur. The damsel bringeth him
on as fast as the knight can go. They had not
ridden far before they came a-nigh, and Perceval
heard the damsel crying aloud for mercy, and
the knight said that mercy upon her he would
not have, and so smote her on the head and
neck with the flat of his sword.

XXV

Perceval espied the knight and saw that the
cognisance of his shield was such as that which
had been set forth to him. 'Sir,' saith he,
'Too churlishly are you entreating this damsel!
What wrong hath she done you?' 'What is
it to you of me and of her?' 'I say it,' saith
Perceval, 'for that no knight ought to do
churlishly to damsel.' 'He will not stint for
you yet!' saith Brundans. He raiseth his
sword and dealeth the damsel a buffet with the
flat so passing heavy that it maketh her stoop
withal so that the blood rayeth out at mouth
and nose. 'By my head,' saith Perceval, 'On
this buffet I defy thee, for the death of Meliot
and for the shame you have done this damsel.'
'Neither you nor none other may brag that you
have heart to attack me, but you shall aby it
right dear!' 'That shall you see presently,'
saith Perceval, and so draweth back the better
to let drive at him, and moveth towards him as
fast as his horse may run, and smiteth him so
passing sore that he pierceth his shield and

bursteth his habergeon and then thrusteth his
spear into his body with such force that he
overthroweth him all in a heap, him and his
horse, in such sort that he breaketh both legs
in the fall.   Then he alighteth over him,
lowereth his coif, unlaceth the ventail, and
smiteth off his head.   'Damsel,' saith he,
'Take it, I present it to you.   And, sith that
you are going to King Arthur's court, I pray
and beseech you that you carry it thither and
so salute him first for me, and tell Messire
Gawain and Lancelot that this is the last
present I look ever to make them, for I think
never to see them more.   Howbeit, wheresoever I may be, I shall be their well-wisher,
nor may I never withdraw me of my love, and
I would fain I might make them the same
present of the heads of all their enemies, but
that I may do nought against God's will.'
The damsel giveth him thanks for that he hath
delivered her from the hands of the knight,
and saith that she shall praise him much thereof
to the King and Messire Gawain.   She goeth
her way and carrieth off the head, and Perceval
biddeth her to God.   He returned back to
Castle Perilous, and the damsel made great joy
thereof when she understood that he had slain
Brundans.   Perceval lay there that night, and
departed on the morrow after that he had
heard mass.   When he came forth of the
castle he met the knight by whom he had
sent the cup to the Sick Knight's wife.
Perceval asketh how it is with him.   'Sir,'
saith he, 'I have carried out your message

right well, for never was a thing received with **Perceval**
such good will.   The Sick Knight hath for- **at**
gone his grudge against his wife.   She eateth **Camelot**
at his table, and the household do her commandment.'   'This liketh me right well,'
saith Perceval, 'and I thank you of doing this
errand.'   'Sir,' saith the knight, 'No thing is
there I would not do for you, for that you
made my brother Knight Hardy there where
you first saw him Knight Coward.'   'Sir,'
saith Perceval, 'Good knight was your brother
and a right good end he made, but a little it
forthinketh me that he might have still been
living had he abided in his cowardize.'   'Sir,'
saith he, 'Better is he dead, sith that he
died with honour, than that he should live with
shame.   Yet glad was I not of his death, for a
hardy knight he was, and yet more would have
been, had he lived longer.'

XXVI

Perceval departeth from the knight and
commendeth him to God.   He hath wandered
so far one day and another that he is returned
to his own most holy castle, and findeth therein
his mother and his sister that the Damsel of
the Car had brought thither.   The Widow
Lady had made bear thither the body that lay
in the coffin before the castle of Camelot in
the rich chapel that she had builded there.
His sister brought the cere-cloth that she took
in the Waste Chapel, and presented there where
the Graal was.   Perceval made bring the coffin
of the other knight that was at the entrance of

his castle, within the chapel likewise, and place
it beside the coffin of his uncle, nor never thereafter might it be removed. Josephus telleth us
that Perceval was in this castle long time, nor
never once moved therefrom in quest of no
adventure; rather was his courage so attorned
to the Saviour of the World and His sweet
Mother, that he and his sister and the damsel
that was therein led a holy life and a religious.
Therein abode they even as it pleased God,
until that his mother passed away and his sister
and all they that were therein save he alone.
The hermits that were nigh the castle buried
them and sang their masses, and came every
day and took counsel of him for the holiness
they saw him do and the good life that he led
there. So one day whilst he was in the holy
chapel where the hallows were, forthwith, behold you, a Voice that cometh down therein:
'Perceval,' saith the Voice, 'Not long shall
you abide herein; wherefore is it God's will
that you dispart the hallows amongst the
hermits of the forest, there where these bodies
shall be served and worshipped, and the most
Holy Graal shall appear herein no more, but
within a brief space shall you know well the
place where it shall be.' When the Voice
departed, all the coffins that were therein
crashed so passing loud that it seemed the
master-hall had fallen. He crosseth and
blesseth him and commendeth him to God.
On a day the hermits came to him. He disparted the holy relics among them, and they
builded above them holy churches and houses

of religion that are seen in the lands and in the **Perceval**
islands. Joseus, the son of King Hermit, **saileth**
remained therein with Perceval, for he well **forth**
knew that he would be departing thence betimes.

XXVII

Perceval heard one day a bell sound loud
and high without the manor toward the sea.
He came to the windows of the hall and saw
the ship come with the white sail and the Red
Cross thereon, and within were the fairest folk
that ever he might behold, and they were all
robed in such manner as though they should
sing mass. When the ship was anchored under
the hall they went to pray in the most holy
chapel. They brought the richest vessels of
gold and silver that any might ever see, like
as it were coffins, and set therein one of the
three bodies of knights that had been brought
into the chapel, and the body of King Fisherman, and of the mother of Perceval. But no
savour in the world smelleth so sweet. Perceval
took leave of Joseus and commended him to
the Saviour of the World, and took leave of
the household, from whom he departed in like
manner. The worshipful men that were in the
ship signed them of the cross and blessed them
likewise. The ship wherein Perceval was drew
far away, and a Voice that issued from the
manor as she departed commended them to God
and to His sweet Mother. Josephus recordeth
us that Perceval departed in such wise, nor
never thereafter did no earthly man know what

Perce-
val's
holy
chapel

became of him, nor doth the history speak of him more. But the history telleth us that Joseus abode in the castle that had been King Fisherman's, and shut himself up therein so that none might enter, and lived upon that the Lord God might send him. He dwelt there long time after that Perceval had departed, and ended therein. After his end, the dwelling began to fall. Natheless never was the chapel wasted nor decayed, but was as whole thereafter as tofore and is so still. The place was far from folk, and the place seemed withal to be somewhat different. When it was fallen into decay, many folk of the lands and islands that were nighest thereunto marvel them what may be in this manor. They dare a many that they should go see what was therein, and sundry folk went thither from all the lands, but none durst never enter there again save two Welsh knights that had heard tell of it. Full comely knights they were, young and joyous-hearted. So either pledged him to other that they would go thither by way of gay adventure; but therein remained they of a long space after, and when again they came forth they led the life of hermits, and clad them in hair shirts, and went by the forest and so ate nought save roots only, and led a right hard life; yet ever they made as though they were glad, and if that any should ask whereof they rejoiced in such-wise, 'Go,' said they to them that asked, 'thither where we have been, and you shall know the wherefore.' In such sort made they answer to the folk. These two knights died in this holy life, nor were none other tidings never brought thence by them.

XXVIII

Here endeth the story of the most Holy
Graal. Josephus, by whom it is placed on
record, giveth the benison of Our Lord to all
that hear and honour it. The Latin from
whence this history was drawn into Romance
was taken in the Isle of Avalon, in a holy
house of religion that standeth at the head of
the Moors Adventurous, there where King
Arthur and Queen Guenievre lie, according to
the witness of the good men religious that are
therein, that have the whole history thereof,
true from the beginning even to the end. After
this same history beginneth the story how Briant
of the Isles renounced King Arthur on account
of Lancelot whom he loved not, and how he
assured King Claudas that reft King Ban of
Benoic of his land. This story telleth how he
conquered him and by what means, and how
Galobrus of the Red Launde came to King
Arthur's court to help Lancelot, for that he
was of his lineage. This story is right long
and right adventurous and weighty, but the
book will now forthwith be silent thereof until
another time.

The Author's Conclusion

For the Lord of Neele made the Lord of
Cambrein this book be written, that never tofore
was treated in Romance but one single time

The worth of this book besides this ; and the book that was made tofore this is so ancient that only with great pains may one make out the letter. And let Messire Johan de Neele well understand that he ought to hold this story dear, nor ought he tell nought thereof to ill-understanding folk, for a good thing that is squandered upon bad folk is never remembered by them for good.

Explicit

the Romance of Perceval the nephew of King Fisherman.

NOTE

*This ancient 'Book of the Holy Graal,' a valuable addition
to our English Arthurian literature, has been translated from
the Old French by Dr. Sebastian Evans. In his 'Epilogue'
the Translator summarises the literary history of the book, and
indicates his strikingly original and noteworthy theory as to
the origin of the work. Whether his views be ultimately
accepted or rejected by Arthurian scholars, Dr. Evans's
noble rendering of the old-world romance will long be
treasured by students for its intrinsic merits. Publisher and
Editor desire to thank him for generously placing his version
at their disposal for inclusion in the present Series. They
desire also to thank Sir Edward Burne-Jones for enriching
the volumes with the embellishments of frontispieces and
title-pages.*

I. G.

Feb. 14th, 1898.

THE
TRANSLATOR'S EPILOGUE

T<small>HIS</small> Book is translated from the first volume The
MSS of *Perceval le Gallois ou le conte du Graal*; edited by M. Ch. Potvin for 'La Société des Bibliophiles Belges' in 1866,[1] from the MS. numbered 11,145 in the library of the Dukes of Burgundy at Brussels. This MS. I find thus described in M. F. J. Marchal's catalogue of that priceless collection: '*Le Roman de Saint Graal*, beginning *Ores lestoires*, in the French language; date, first third of the sixteenth century; with ornamental capitals.'[2] Written three centuries later than the original romance, and full as it is of faults of the scribe, this manuscript is by far the most complete known copy of the Book of the Graal in existence, being defective only in Branch XXI. Titles 8 and 9, the substance of which is fortunately preserved elsewhere. Large fragments, however, amounting in all to nearly one-seventh of

---

[1] 6 vols. 8vo. Mons, 1866-1871.

[2] Marchal *Cat.*, 2 vols. Brussels, 1842. Vol. i. p. 223.

M. Potvin's edition the whole, of a copy in handwriting of the thirteenth century, are preserved in six consecutive leaves and one detached leaf bound up with a number of other works in a MS. numbered 113 in the City Library at Berne. The volume is in folio on vellum closely written in three columns to the page, and the seven leaves follow the last poem contained in it, entitled *Duremart le Gallois.* The manuscript is well known, having been lent to M. de Sainte Palaye for use in the Monuments of French History issued by the Benedictines of the Congregation of St. Maur. Selections from the poems it contains are given in Sinner's *Extraits de Poésie du XIII. Siècle,*[1] and it is described, unfortunately without any reference to these particular leaves, by the same learned librarian in the *Catalogus Codicum* MSS. *Bibl. Bernensis.* J. R. Sinner.[2]

M. Potvin has carefully collated for his edition all that is preserved of the Romance in this manuscript, comprising all the beginning of the work as far as Branch III. Title 8, about the middle, and from Branch XVIII. Title 23, near the beginning, to Branch XIX. Title 5, in the middle. Making allowance for variations

[1] Lausanne, 1759.
[2] 3 vols. 8vo. Berne, 1770, etc. Vol. ii., Introduc. viii and p. 389 *et seq.*

of spelling and sundry minor differences of reading, by no means always in favour of the earlier scribe, the Berne fragments are identical with the corresponding portions of the Brussels manuscript, and it is therefore safe to assume that the latter is on the whole an accurate transcript of the entire original Romance.

The only note of time in the book itself is contained in the declaration at the end. From this it appears that it was written by order of the Seingnor of Cambrein for Messire Jehan the Seingnor of Neele. M. Potvin, without giving any reason for so doing, assumes that this Lord of Cambrein is none other than the Bishop of Cambrai. If this assumption be correct, the person referred to was probably either John of Béthune, who held the see from 1200 till July 27, 1219, or his successor Godfrey of Fontaines (Condé), who held it till 1237. To me, however, it seems more likely that the personage intended was in reality the 'Seingnor' of Cambrin, the chef-lieu of a canton of the same name, on a small hill over-looking the peat-marshes of Béthune, albeit I can find no other record of any such landed proprietor's existence.

Be this as it may, the Messire Jehan, Seingnor of Neele, can hardly be other than the John de Nesle who was present at the

(margin note: Date of the Romance)

The Welsh translation battle of Bouvines in 1214, and who in 1225 sold the lordship of Bruges to Joan of Flanders.[1] These dates therefore may be regarded as defining that of the original Romance within fairly narrow limits.

This conclusion is confirmed by other evidence. An early Welsh translation of the story was published with an English version and a glossary by the Rev. Robert Williams in the first volume of his *Selections from the Hengwrt* mss.[2] The first volume of this work is entitled *Y Seint Greal, being the adventures of King Arthur's knights of the Round Table, in the quest of the Holy Grail, and on other occasions. Originally written about the year* 1200. The volume, following the manuscript now in the library of W. W. E. Wynne, Esq., at Peniarth, is divided into two parts. The first, fol. 1-109 of the manuscript, represents the thirteenth to the seventeenth book of Sir Thomas Malory's *Morte D'Arthur*. Of the second, which represents the Romance here translated, Mr. Williams writes: 'The second portion of the Welsh Greal, folios 110-280, contains the adventures of Gwalchmei Peredur and Lancelot, and of the knights of the Round Table;

[1] Rigord. *Chron.* 196, p. 288. Wm. le Breton, *Phil.* xi. 547. See also Birch-Hirschfeld, *Die Gralsage*, p. 143.
[2] 2 vols. 8vo. London, Richards, 1876-1892.

but these are not found in the *Morte D'Arthur.*
The Peniarth MS. is beautifully written on
vellum, and in perfect preservation, and its date
is that of Henry VI., the early part of the
fifteenth century. The orthography and style
of writing agrees literally with that of the
Mabinogion of the Llyvr Côch Hergest, which
is of that date. This, of course, is a transcript
of an earlier copy; but there is no certainty
when it was first translated into Welsh, though
Aneurin Owen in his Catalogue of the Hengwrt
MSS. assigns it to the sixth year of Henry I.
It is mentioned by Davydh ab Gwilym, who
died in 1368.'

Whatever may be the date of the Welsh
version, the translator had no great mastery of
French, and is often at fault as to the meaning
both of words and sentences, and when in a
difficulty is only too apt to cut the knot by
omitting the passage bodily. The book itself,
moreover, is not entire. On page 275, all
between Branch IX. Title 16 and Branch XI.
Title 2, twenty-two chapters in all, is missing.
Again, on page 355, Titles 10-16 in Branch
XXI. are left out, while the whole of the last
Branch, containing 28 Titles, is crumpled up
into one little chapter, from which it would seem
that the Welshman had read the French, but
thought it waste of pains to translate it. In all,

The Welsh names not to speak of other defects, there are fifty-six whole chapters in the present book, of which there is not a word in the Welsh.

In one matter, however, Mr. Williams's English translation has stood me in good stead. In Branch xxi., as I have said, the French manuscript makes default of two Titles, but almost the whole of their substance is supplied by the Welsh version. By an unlucky accident, before the hiatus in the French is fully filled up, the Welsh version itself becomes defective, though the gap thus left open can hardly extend beyond a very few words. Without this supplement, incomplete as it is, it would have been impossible to give the full drift of one of the Romancer's best stories, which is equally unintelligible in both the French and Welsh texts in their present state.

As the Welsh version gives a number of names both of persons and places widely differing from those in the French, it may be useful here to note the principal changes made. Perceval in the Welsh is called Peredur, which is said to mean *steel suit*. The Welshman, however, adds that the name in French is *Peneffresvo Galief*, which, unless it be a misreading or miswriting for Perceval le Galois, is to me wholly unintelligible. Perceval's father, Alain li Gros, is in the Welsh Earl

Evrawg, and his sister Dindrane, Danbrann. An ill-sorted union
King Arthur is Emperor Arthur, his Queen
Guenievre, Gwenhwyvar, and their son Lohot,
Lohawt or Llacheu. Messire Gawain is
Gwalchmei; Chaus, son of Ywain li Aoutres,
Gawns, son of Owein Vrych; Messire Kay or
Kex is Kei the Long; Ahuret the Bastard,
Anores; Ygerne, wife of Uther Pendragon,
Eigyr; Queen Jandree, Landyr; and King
Fisherman for the most part King Peleur. Of
places, Cardoil is Caerlleon on Usk, Pannenoi-
sance, Penvoisins; Tintagel, Tindagoyl; and
Avalon, Avallach.

By a double stroke of ill-luck, the complete
and wholly independent Romance here translated has thus been printed by its two former
editors as if it were only a part of some other
story. M. Potvin describes it as the ' First
Part, the Romance in Prose,' of his *Perceval le
Gallois,* and Mr. Williams accepts it as the
' Second Portion ' of his *Y Seint Greal.* This
unhappy collocation has led not a few of M.
Potvin's readers to neglect his First Part, under
the impression that the story is retold in the
other volumes containing the Romance in verse;
while not a few of Mr. Williams's readers have
neglected his Second Portion under the impression that there could be nothing of any special
importance in an adjunct referred to by the

Fulke Fitz-Warine Editor in so perfunctory a manner. In very truth, however, the Story of the Holy Graal here told is not only the most coherent and poetic of all the many versions of the Legend, but is also the first and most authentic.

This seems to be proved beyond doubt by a passage in the History of Fulke Fitz-Warine, originally written apparently between the years 1256 and 1264. The passage occurs at the end of the History, and is printed in verse of which I give a literal prose translation.

'Merlin saith that in Britain the Great a Wolf shall come from the White Launde. Twelve sharp teeth shall he have, six below and six above. He shall have so fierce a look that he shall chase the Leopard forth of the White Launde, so much force shall he have and great virtue. We now know that Merlin said this for Fulke the son of Waryn, for each of you ought to understand of a surety how in the time of the King Arthur that was called the White Launde which is now named the White Town. For in this country was the chapel of S. Austin that was fair, where Kahuz, the son of Ywein, dreamed that he carried off the candlestick and that he met a man who hurt him with a knife and wounded him in the side. And he, on sleep, cried out so loud that King Arthur hath heard him and awakened from sleep. And when Kahuz was awake, he put his hand to his side. There hath he found the knife that had smitten him through. So TELLETH US THE GRAAL, THE BOOK OF THE HOLY VESSEL. There the King Arthur recovered his bounty and his valour when he had lost all his chivalry and his virtue. From this country issued forth the Wolf as saith Merlin the Wise, and the twelve sharp teeth have we known by his shield. He bore a shield indented as the heralds have devised. In the shield are twelve teeth of gules and argent. By the Leopard may be known and well-understood King John, for he bore in his shield the leopards of beaten gold.' [1]

The story of Kahuz or Chaus here indicated by the historian is told at length in the opening chapters of the present work and, so far as is known, nowhere else. The inference is therefore unavoidable that we have here 'The Graal, the Book of the Holy Vessel' to which the biographer of Fulke refers. The use, more-

---

[1] *L'histoire de Foulkes Fitz-Warin.* Ed. F. Michel, Paris, 1840; p. 110. Ed. T. Wright (Warton Club), London, 1855; p. 179. Ed. J. Stevenson (*Rolls Pub. Chron.* of R. Coggeshall), London, 1875; p. 412. The MS. containing the history (*MS. Reg.* 12. c. XII.) was first privately printed for the late Sir T. Duffus Hardy from a transcript by A. Berbrugger.

The over, of the definite article shows that the
trouveur writer held this book to be conclusive authority
Sarrazin on the subject. By the time he retold the story
of Fulke, a whole library of Romances about
Perceval and the Holy Graal had been written,
with some of which it is hard to believe that
any historian of the time was unacquainted.
He nevertheless distinguishes this particular
story as 'The Graal,' a way of speaking he
would scarce have adopted had he known of
any other 'Graals' of equal or nearly equal
authority.

Several years later, about 1280, the trouveur
Sarrazin also cites 'The Graal' (*li Graaus*) in
the same manner, in superfluous verification of
the then accepted truism that King Arthur was
at one time Lord of Great Britain. This
appeal to 'The Graal' as the authority for a
general belief shows that it was at that time
recognised as a well-spring of authentic knowledge; while the fact that the trouveur was not
confounding 'The Graal' with the later version
of the story is further shown by his going on
presently to speak of 'the Romance that
Chrestien telleth so fairly of Perceval—the
adventures of the Graal.'[1]

[1] 'Le Roman de Ham,' in the Appendix to F. Michel's
Histoire des Ducs de Normandie. Soc. de l'Hist. de France,
1840, pp. 225, 230.

Perhaps, however, the most striking testimony to the fact that this work is none other than the original Book of the Graal is to be found in the Chronicle of Helinand, well known at the time the Romance was written not only as a historian but as a troubadour at one time in high favour at the court of Philip Augustus, and in later years as one of the most ardent preachers of the Albigensian Crusade. The passage, a part of which has been often quoted, is inserted in the Chronicle under the year 720, and runs in English thus:

'At this time a certain marvellous vision was revealed by an angel to a certain hermit in Britain concerning S. Joseph, the decurion who deposed from the cross the Body of Our Lord, as well as concerning the paten or dish in the which Our Lord supped with His disciples, whereof the history was written out by the said hermit and is called "Of the Graal" (*de Gradali*). Now, a platter, broad and somewhat deep, is called in French *gradalis* or *gradale*, wherein costly meats with their sauce are wont to be set before rich folk by degrees (*gradatim*) one morsel after another in divers orders, and in the vulgar speech it is called *graalz*, for that it is grateful and acceptable to him that eateth therein, as well for that which containeth the victual, for that haply it is of silver or other

precious material, as for the contents thereof, to
wit, the manifold courses of costly meats. I
have not been able to find this history written
in Latin, but it is in the possession of certain
noblemen written in French only, nor, as they
say, can it easily be found complete. This,
however, I have not hitherto been able to obtain
from any person so as to read it with attention.
As soon as I can do so, I will translate into
Latin such passages as are more useful and more
likely to be true.' [1]

A comparison of this passage with the Intro-
duction to the present work [2] leaves no doubt
that Helinand here refers to this Book of the
Graal, which cannot therefore be of a later date
than that at which he made this entry in his
chronicle. At the same time, the difficulty he
experienced in obtaining even the loan of the
volume shows that the work had at that time
been only lately written, as in the course of a
few years, copies of a book so widely popular

[1] Helinandi Op. Ed. Migne. *Patrol.* Vol. ccxii. col.
814. The former part of the passage is quoted with due
acknowledgment by Vincent of Beauvais. *Spec. Hist.*
B. xxiii. c. 147. Vincent, however, spells the French
word '*grail*,' and, by turning Helinand's *nec* into *nunc*,
makes him say that the French work can *now* easily be
found complete. Vincent finished his *Speculum Historiale*
in 1244. B. xxi. c. 105.

[2] Vol. i. p. 1, etc.

must have been comparatively common. The **Vincent**
date, therefore, at which Helinand's Chronicle **of Beau-**
was written determines approximately that of **vais**
the Book of the Graal.

In its present state, the Chronicle comes to an
end with a notice of the capture of Constantin-
ople by the French in 1204, and it has been
hastily assumed that Helinand's labours as a
chronicler must have closed in that year. As a
matter of fact they had not then even begun.
At that time Helinand was still a courtly
troubadour, and had not yet entered on the
monastic career during which his Chronicle
was compiled. He was certainly living as late
as 1229, and preached a sermon, which assuredly
shows no signs of mental decrepitude, in that
year at a synod in Toulouse.[1]

Fortunately a passage in the *Speculum Historiale* of Vincent of Beauvais, himself a younger
contemporary and probably a personal acquaintance of Helinand, throws considerable light on

---

[1] Sermon xxvi., printed in Migne, u. s. col. 692. It
has been doubted whether this sermon, preached in the
church of S. Jacques, was addressed to the Council held
at Toulouse in 1219, or to the one held in 1229, but a
perusal of the sermon itself decides the question. It is
wholly irrelevant to the topics discussed at the former
gathering, while it is one continued commentary on the
business transacted at the latter. See also Dom Brial,
Hist. Litt. de la France, xviii. 92.

the real date of Helinand's Chronicle. After recounting certain matters connected with the early years of the thirteenth century, the last date mentioned being 1209, Vincent proceeds:—

'In those times, in the diocese of Beauvais, was Helinand monk of Froid-mont, a man religious and distinguished for his eloquence, who also composed those verses on Death in our vulgar tongue which are publicly read, so elegantly and so usefully that the subject is laid open clearer than the light. He also diligently digested into a certain huge volume a Chronicle from the beginning of the world down to his own time. But in truth this work was dissipated and dispersed in such sort that it is nowhere to be found entire. For it is reported that the said Helinand lent certain sheets of the said work to one of his familiars, to wit, Guarin, Lord Bishop of Senlis of good memory, and thus, whether through forgetfulness or negligence or some other cause, lost them altogether. From this work, however, as far as I have been able to find it, I have inserted many passages in this work of mine own also.'

It will thus be seen that about 1209, Helinand became a monk at Froid-mont, and it is exceedingly improbable that any portion of his Chronicle was written before that date. On the other hand, his 'familiar' Guarin only became Bishop of Senlis in 1214, and died in 1227,[1] so that it is certain Helinand wrote the last part of his Chronicle not later than the last-mentioned year. The limits of time, therefore, between which the Chronicle was written are clearly circumscribed; and if it is impossible to define the exact year in which this particular entry was made, it is not, I fancy, beyond the legitimate bounds of critical conjecture.

On the first page of the Romance, Helinand read that an Angel had appeared to a certain hermit in Britain and revealed to him the history of the Holy Graal. In transferring the record of this event to his Chronicle, he was compelled by the exigencies of his system, which required the insertion of every event recorded under some particular year, to assign a date to the occurrence. A vague 'five hundred years ago' would be likely to suggest itself as an appropriate time at which the occurrence might be supposed to have taken place; and if he were writing in 1220, the revelation to the hermit would thus naturally be relegated to the year 720, the year under which the entry actually appears. This, of course, is pure guesswork, but the fact remains that the Chronicle was written in or about 1220, and the Book of the Graal not long before it.

[1] *De Mas Latrie. Trés. de Chron.*, col. 1488.

Master Blihis The name of the author is nowhere recorded. He may possibly be referred to in the 'Elucidation' prefixed to the rhymed version of *Percival le Gallois* under the name of 'Master Blihis,' but this vague and tantalising pseudonym affords no hint of his real identity.[1] Whoever he may have been, I hope that I am not misled by a translator's natural partiality for the author he translates in assigning him a foremost rank among the masters of mediæval prose romance.

With these testimonies to its age and genuineness, I commend the Book of the Graal to all who love to read of King Arthur and his knights of the Table Round. They will find here printed in English for the first time what I take to be in all good faith the original story of Sir Perceval and the Holy Graal, whole and incorrupt as it left the hands of its first author.

SEBASTIAN EVANS.

Coombe Lea, Bickley, Kent,
January 1898.

---

[1] Cf. Potvin, *P. le G.* ii. 1 and 7, with vol. i. p. 131 and vol. ii. p. 112 of the present work.

www.ingramcontent.com/pod-product-compliance
Lightning Source LLC
Chambersburg PA
CBHW031408270326
41929CB00010BA/1378